D1384310

FIGHTING CENSORSHIP
New York Times v. United States

D. J. HERDA

Enslow Publishing
101 W. 23rd Street
Suite 240
New York, NY 10011
USA
enslow.com

Published in 2017 by Enslow Publishing, LLC.
101 W. 23rd Street, Suite 240, New York, NY 10011

Library of Congress Cataloging-in-Publication Data

Names: Herda, D. J., 1948–, author.
Title: Fighting censorship : New York Times v. United States / D.J. Herda.
Description: New York : Enslow Publishing, 2017. | Series: US Supreme Court
landmark cases | Includes bibliographical references and index.
Identifiers: LCCN 2016026255 | ISBN 9780766084322 (library bound)
Subjects: LCSH: New York Times Company—Trials, litigation, etc.—Juvenile
literature. | United States—Trials, litigation, etc.—Juvenile
literature. | Freedom of the press—United States—Juvenile literature. |
Censorship—United States—Juvenile literature. | Pentagon
Papers—Juvenile literature. | Security classification (Government
documents)—United States—Juvenile literature.
Classification: LCC KF228.N52 H465 2017 | DDC 342.7308/53—dc23
LC record available at https://lccn.loc.gov/2016026255

Printed in Malaysia

To Our Readers: We have done our best to make sure all websites in this book were active and
appropriate when we went to press. However, the author and the publisher have no control over and
assume no liability for the material available on those websites or on any websites they may link to.
Any comments or suggestions can be sent by e-mail to customerservice@enslow.com.

Portions of this book originally appeared in the book *New York Times v. United States:
National Security and Censorship, Revised Edition.*

Photo Credits: Cover Walter Bennett/The LIFE Picture Collection/Getty Images; p. 4 University of
Texas Libraries; pp. 15, 18, 25, 46, 54, 64 © AP Images; p. 29 NARA, downloaded from Wikimedia
Commons/File:Nixon Official Presidential Portrait, 07-08-1971restoredh.jpg; p. 36 Hulton
Archive/Getty Images; pp. 69, 87 Bettmann/Getty Images; p. 80 Dirck Halstead/The LIFE Images
Collection/Getty Images; p. 82 A 1971 Herblock Cartoon, © The Herb Block Foundation.

Contents

Vietnam

— International boundary
—·— Province boundary
★ National capital
⊙ Province capital
╬ Railroad
— Road
--- Trail

| 0 | 50 | 100 Kilometers |
| 0 | 50 | 100 Miles |

Boundary representation is not
necessarily authoritative. Names
in Vietnam are shown without
diacritical marks.

Base 800471 (546744) 12-85

The Vietnam War

T he Southeastern Asian country of Vietnam was part of Imperial China for more than a thousand years, from 111 BC to AD 939. In that year, following a Vietnamese victory in the Battle of Bach Dang River, the independent state of Vietnam was born. After that, numerous Vietnamese royal dynasties flourished as the young nation grew geographically, expanding its political influence throughout Southeast Asia. Today, the small nation is the 14th most populous country in the world with more than 90 million people.

A Battle-Torn Nation

War was nothing new to the battle-torn nation. Vietnam had been at war for most of its history. Finally, in the 1800s, Vietnam had settled into an uneasy partnership between three countries:

On this map, Vietnam is colored beige. You can see it is narrow and runs along the eastern coast of the Indochina Peninsula.

Annam and Tonkin in the north and Cochinchina in the south. But Vietnam's independence was stripped by France in a series of military conquests between 1859 and 1885. In 1862, the southern third of the country became the French colony of Cochinchina. By 1884, the entire country of Vietnam had come under French rule and was formally integrated into the union of French Indochina in 1887.

During the Second World War, the Japanese invaded Vietnam, occupying it and robbing it of its natural resources to help fuel Japan's ever-hungry war machine. Japan completed its takeover in 1945. When the War ended, the French returned and resumed control of the nation.

Finally, in 1945, a well-armed group of Indochinese, known as the Viet Minh and led by a Soviet-trained Communist named Ho Chi Minh, forced the Annamese emperor Bao Dai off the throne. The group promptly claimed Annam, Tonkin, and Cochinchina as its own. Ho Chi Minh was made president of the new country, which was renamed the Republic of Vietnam.

But British forces in Cochinchina, reinforced by French troops in October 1945, soon drove the Viet Minh out of the South. The following June, France claimed Cochinchina as a republic of the French Union, naming Bao Dai as chief of state. Soon, fighting broke out once more between French and Viet Minh forces. Communist China, the Soviet Union, and other Communist countries supported Ho Chi Minh's Viet Minh troops from the North. On the other side, Great Britain, the United States, and several other Democratic countries supported Bao Dai's new government in the South. Meanwhile, Dai appointed Ngo Dinh Diem his new premier.

After nearly a decade of civil war, the fighting between the North and the South finally came to a halt on July 21, 1954. Following a long and complicated peace conference held in Geneva, Switzerland, an arbitrary "line" was drawn across Vietnam. Ho Chi Minh would control the government in the North, and Bao Dai would retain control of the government in the South. The Geneva Accords also called for national elections to unite the two governments into one country. But when South Vietnam (as it was referred to then) rejected North Vietnam's proposals to arrange for the elections, fighting once again broke out between the two nations.

The US Gets Involved

By the end of his term of office in 1961, US President Dwight D. Eisenhower was becoming increasingly concerned about the escalating war in Asia. He had received several classified military documents detailing the Soviet Union's military involvement in the country of Laos, which neighbors Vietnam. A small, well-armed group of North Vietnamese troops, called Viet Cong, slowly began infiltrating South Vietnam. The group was using its bases in Laos to stage attacks against the government of South Vietnam. The Viet Cong's goal was to win the support of the people, overthrow the government of Ngo Dinh Diem, and unite South Vietnam with North Vietnam under Communist rule. And it seemed as though the

Viet Cong were winning. Unless the United States acted to stop the North Vietnamese, all of Southeast Asia might soon fall to Communism. At least that was the theory.

When John F. Kennedy won the presidential election in 1960, he met with outgoing President Eisenhower for a briefing on the war in Vietnam. At Eisenhower's suggestion, Kennedy agreed to send additional US advisers and increase economic aid to South Vietnam to help the democratic government—now headed by Ngo Dinh Diem—defeat the North Vietnamese forces.

But despite increased US aid, the Viet Minh—now called the Viet Cong—continued their advances, slowly winning control of many of the small towns that dotted the South Vietnamese countryside. In order to stop the spread of Communism, Kennedy had to stop the Viet Cong. In a speech to the American people early in 1961, the American president called Vietnam "a proving ground for democracy" and a "test of American responsibility and determination."[1] Few Americans at the time had even heard of Vietnam, and fewer still cared about what was happening there.

A Growing Problem

Following his speech, the president called his closest advisers to a meeting to discuss the growing Vietnamese problem. Half of the advisers suggested that the United States continue sending Ngo Dinh Diem aid. The other half wanted the president to send US combat troops to help in the fighting. Kennedy himself was not prepared to abandon Vietnam to Communist forces, but neither was he ready to commit American troops to a war halfway around the world.[2] Besides, Congress would never authorize such an ambitious military venture, and he might not win support for the plan from the American people.

So in April 1961, Kennedy created a special task force to provide social, economic, political, and military aid to the South Vietnamese government. He agreed to support the strengthening of South Vietnam's army of one hundred fifty thousand soldiers with an additional twenty thousand men. He also agreed to send an additional one hundred American military advisers to Vietnam, bringing the total number of Americans in that country to eight hundred.

The following month, Kennedy asked Vice President Lyndon B. Johnson to go on a fact-finding mission to Saigon, the capital of South Vietnam. There, after meeting with President Ngo Dinh Diem, Johnson learned just how serious the war was. Upon his return to America, the vice president—who opposed the spread of Communism as much as Kennedy did—announced that the loss of Vietnam to the Communists would one day force America to fight "on the beaches of Waikiki [Hawaii]."

Johnson said, "The battle against communism must be joined in Southeast Asia with strength and determination … or the United States, inevitably, must surrender the Pacific and take up our defenses on our own shores."[3]

Meanwhile, Ngo Dinh Diem proposed to Kennedy that the United States support a plan to increase South Vietnam's military to two hundred thousand soldiers. That would mean more American advisers, more United States equipment, and more economic aid. In response, Kennedy sent one of his most highly regarded generals, Maxwell Taylor, to Saigon to study the situation more closely.

Upon his return, Taylor sent a classified message to Kennedy. In it he suggested that Kennedy send three squadrons of helicopters, manned by US pilots, plus eight thousand soldiers acting as "advisers" to Vietnam. By having the soldiers pose as advisers, the United States could hold public knowledge of its military involvement in Vietnam to a minimum. That would be necessary partly to avoid a negative reaction from Congress and the American voters, and partly to comply with the provisions of the Geneva Accords. The Geneva Accords are international agreements that strictly prohibit military intervention in foreign countries.

Playing down the possibility that such action might lead to a long and drawn-out war between North Vietnam and the United States, Taylor went on to write,

> North Vietnam is extremely vulnerable to conventional bombing. ... There is no case for fearing a mass onslaught of communist manpower into South Vietnam and its neighboring states [Laos and Cambodia], particularly if our air power is allowed a free hand against logistical targets.[4]

Although still cautious about pouring massive quantities of US aid and troops into Vietnam, Kennedy knew that he had to do something. Despite his outright denials to the American public, the president approved the transfer to South Vietnam of several thousand more "advisers" backed by several hundred American pilots. The pilots were to begin flying secret combat missions out of Bien Hoa, an air base just north of Saigon. The real purpose of the flights would be carefully disguised as training exercises for the South Vietnamese army.

Meanwhile, growing numbers of Washington-based agencies were keeping tabs on the developing Vietnamese war. They conducted detailed studies of the conflict as it unfolded, and they reached the conclusion that South Vietnam was winning. The Communist regime, based in the North Vietnamese capital of Hanoi, could not possibly emerge victorious against the combined forces of South Vietnam and the military might of the United States. At least that is what the studies showed. But while all the studies and reports pointed to an eventual victory for South Vietnam, they failed to take into account one very important fact—the determination of the North Vietnamese people—the Communists—to win.

That determination showed itself in January 1963 at the Battle of Ap Bac. There, South Vietnamese and US troops attacked a small group of North Vietnamese soldiers and their supporters. Despite being outnumbered ten to one, the North Vietnamese not only held their ground but also forced their attackers to turn back—killing several South Vietnamese soldiers and three American helicopter crew members in the process.

Ap Bac proved to be an embarrassment to Kennedy. So, too, did the American news media, which was beginning to pose indelicate questions to the US administration—questions such as why had the South Vietnamese lost to an undermanned army and what were American pilots doing in the battle? Kennedy, who was well skilled at sidestepping the press's most embarrassing questions, could have imposed censorship on the media, thus preventing them from reporting *all* US involvement in Vietnam, but that action would imply that there was a larger war going on than Kennedy was willing to admit.

Instead, Kennedy continued to deny American involvement. In the meantime, he continued pouring more aid into Vietnam, assuming—as did his staff—that larger quantities of people, money, and material would produce greater results. Kennedy, of course, turned out to be wrong and even admitted so to one of his administrative assistants, Kenneth O'Donnell. O'Donnell said that Kennedy had told him he planned to withdraw all American troops from Vietnam after his presidential reelection in 1964.

But Kennedy was not given that opportunity. He would be killed by an assassin's bullet in 1963—less than one year before the upcoming national election.

Johnson Takes the Helm

Following the assassination, Kennedy was succeeded to the presidency by Vice President Lyndon B. Johnson. Johnson, a Texas-born millionaire, was a large man whose wildly swinging moods matched his size. At times, according to author Stanley Karnow, Johnson could be "cruel and kind, violent and gentle, petty, generous, cunning, naive, crude, candid, and frankly dishonest."[5]

One thing that Johnson was *not* was soft on Communism. America, he firmly believed, was the beacon of liberty—a philosophy Johnson had inherited from studying the daring Battle of the Alamo, which took place in 1836. At the Alamo, a ragtag band of Texans fought to their deaths in an effort to gain independence from Mexico.

So, on November 24, 1963, only two days after Kennedy's assassination, Johnson instructed his aide Henry Cabot Lodge to "tell those generals in Saigon that Lyndon Johnson intends to stand by our word." Johnson then wrote a memo to the National Security Council, stating that the United States would help South Vietnam "win their contest against the externally directed and supported Communist conspiracy."[6]

Meanwhile, in South Vietnam, President Ngo Dinh Diem had been killed only weeks earlier in a political coup (an uprising) against the government by former supporters who had turned against him. Ngo Dinh Diem was replaced by a military council of South Vietnamese generals. The generals were eventually replaced by General Nguyen Khanh.

Anxious to learn more about the rapidly unraveling political situation in South Vietnam, Johnson sent Secretary of Defense Robert McNamara to Saigon. Upon his return, McNamara publicly boasted about how well South Vietnam was doing in its war against the North and Ho Chi Minh. But in a secret memo deliberately withheld from the press, the defense secretary reported to Johnson that the situation in South Vietnam was "disturbing." He predicted that, unless the United States took immediate and strong action, South Vietnam could very well fall to the northern Communists. He based his findings on the fact that the South Vietnamese army was losing more weapons to the North Vietnamese than it was capturing. The North Vietnamese also controlled more of the country's people and held more territory than Washington had previously believed.

Meanwhile, the Joint Chiefs of Staff—the military leaders who lead America's armed forces—issued a statement to Johnson declaring that South Vietnam was a key to America's world leadership. If the United States could not defeat Communism in Asia, they warned, it would not be able to stop it in Africa or Latin America. In order to win, the leaders concluded, the United States had to expand the war into neighboring North Vietnam, Cambodia, and Laos. Johnson, though hesitant to expand the war and distrustful by nature of most military men, reluctantly agreed.

By now Americans had come to realize that a real war was being waged in South Vietnam. American reporters were sending stories back to the United States daily, and television and radio crews combed Southeast Asia looking for dramatic accounts of brave American soldiers locked in deadly battle with the Communists from North Vietnam.

By mid-1964, the total number of Americans living and working in South Vietnam topped one hundred thousand. The Americans taught the South Vietnamese how to breed pigs,

These troops wade through a swampy creek during a 1965 search-and-destroy mission to find guerilla hideouts in the jungles about 40 miles (64 km) northeast of Saigon.

dig freshwater wells, and build better houses. They worked as doctors, school teachers, accountants, and mechanics. They even established an American radio station in Saigon. At the same time, the Central Intelligence Agency (CIA) and a dozen other undercover agencies—among which there was one whose duties included spying on other spies—were hard at work trying to uncover North Vietnam's plans to win the war.

Following his landslide presidential victory at the polls in November 1964, Johnson believed he finally had the support of the American people to expand US involvement in the war in South Vietnam. By introducing massive American air and sea strikes against North Vietnam and bolstering the number of American ground troops already fighting in the South, he was convinced that he could bring the North Vietnamese government to its knees.

But Johnson learned the hard way, over the next four years, that an ever-increasing supply of arms and soldiers does not automatically result in military victory. By March 31, 1968, when Johnson announced that he would not seek a second full term as president, the North Vietnamese had still not been humbled. And the war that had now outlived the administrations of two American presidents raged on.

Nixon Makes a Promise

In 1968, Republican candidate Richard M. Nixon—like Johnson and Kennedy, a strong opponent of the spread of Communism throughout Asia—ran for president on the promise that he had a secret plan to end the war in Vietnam. The United States, he insisted, would not only win, it would win with dignity and honor. Nixon's long political history, solid background as vice president under Dwight D. Eisenhower, and his promise to end the war helped him to win a closely contested victory in November. Now an anxious America waited for Nixon to make good on his promise.

Armed with recent information that 40,000 North Vietnamese troops were using bases in neighboring Cambodia, Nixon decided to act. On March 16, 1969, he met with

Presidential Assistant for National Security Affairs Henry Kissinger, Secretary of State William P. Rogers, and Secretary of Defense Melvin R. Laird. He told them that the "only way" to get the Communists to negotiate an honorable end to the war was "to do something on the military front … something they will understand."[7] The very next day American planes began bombing Cambodia.

The bombings were a well-guarded secret from the start. The United States did not want to admit that it was attacking a foreign country whose neutrality it claimed to respect. The other countries involved in the military action played along with the United States. Cambodia's Prince Norodom Sihanouk, fearful of losing his own rule and anxious to have the North Vietnamese removed from his land, said nothing of the raids for fear American would stop them before the job was done. North Vietnam's Ho Chi Minh, not wanting to admit that the North Vietnamese had crossed the borders of their neighbor and were living and working in Cambodia, also did not complain.

But there was another reason for Nixon's secrecy about the Cambodian campaign—there was a growing anti-war sentiment in the United States. Nixon knew that if the bombings were made public, hundreds of thousands of Americans already tired of the war might rebel. Anti-war protestors were already marching on the Capitol and throughout the streets of America. Nixon mistakenly believed that by keeping news of the bombings from the American public, he could win the war that much faster.[8]

Some 30–35,000 marchers paraded down New York's Fifth Avenue to demand an end to US involvement in the Vietnam War.

A Secret War

When a reporter for the *New York Times* learned about the Cambodian affair and wrote an article detailing the "secret war" being waged there, Americans began to revolt. Violent demonstrations erupted from coast to coast. Nixon was furious with the *New York Times* for releasing the story. The last thing he needed were more anti-war protests at home.

On May 14, in an effort to satisfy both Congress and the American people, Nixon delivered his first major television address on the subject of Vietnam. He told the nation that he had developed a proposal for a negotiated settlement to end the fighting and bring American troops home. He appealed for patience, saying, "[T]he time has come for new initiatives."[9] Shortly thereafter, he announced a program for the gradual withdrawal of a small number of American troops from South Vietnam. The following September he announced a second troop withdrawal, and in a televised address on November 3, he told the nation about a cooperative United States-South Vietnam plan to bring *all* US troops home and turn the fighting back over to the South Vietnamese.

Secretly, Nixon hoped that the announced withdrawals would convince the North Vietnamese that the United States was serious about ending the war. He also hoped the announcement would encourage them to come to the peace table, where he was convinced an honorable solution to the conflict could be worked out. But his plan was not to be.

Following the president's announcement of troop withdrawals, Ho Chi Minh assembled his advisers to devise a plan that would sweep North Vietnam to victory. The North Vietnamese had long assumed that they could "outwait" the United States for an end to the war. Now they decided the time was right to return to the use of the small bands of guerrilla fighters that had earlier proved so effective in invading South Vietnam. Ho Chi Minh addressed his nation over Radio Hanoi, warning his people that, despite Nixon's announcement of troop withdrawals, the war in the South was gearing up. The North Vietnamese people, he said, had to "be prepared to fight many years more" until the American enemy "gives up his aggressive design."[10]

As the war in South Vietnam heated up, Nixon decided to attack additional Communist strongholds in Cambodia, this time using land forces. On the evening of April 30, 1970, as he addressed the nation about his new Cambodian "incursion" (attack), a US and South Vietnamese force of twenty thousand men supported by American aircraft launched an attack against two major North Vietnamese bases in Cambodia.

The plan was a disaster from the start. Instead of finding tens of thousands of Communist soldiers in the camps, the drive netted little more than US frustration. Most of the North Vietnamese, having learned in advance of the pending attack, had fled Cambodia weeks earlier and were hard at work shifting their center of operations to the northernmost provinces of South Vietnam. The Communists who remained were forced deeper into Cambodia, ultimately destabilizing the nation. Despite his promise to the American people that the peace they were seeking was in sight, Nixon had merely succeeded in lengthening the war.

Growing Anti-War Movement

Meanwhile, the anti-war movement at home continued to grow. The press lashed out at Nixon, who reporters said had gone back on his pledge to end the war. Throughout the entire country, teachers, lawyers, businesspeople, and clergy joined forces with students to protest the continuing war. The demonstrations came to a head on May 4, 1970, when protesting students at Ohio's Kent State University were met by members of Ohio's National Guard. Several guard members panicked, firing into a "rock-throwing mob," according to some sources at the time, killing four youths.

The slayings sparked protests across the country. More than four hundred colleges and universities shut down as students and professors alike staged strikes. Nearly a hundred thousand demonstrators marched on Washington, encircling the White House and demanding Nixon's impeachment.

After a year and a half in office, Nixon—who had campaigned for the presidency on a pledge to "end the war and win the peace"—found himself more deeply embroiled than ever. And his problems had only begun.

CHAPTER 2

The Pentagon Papers

Nicknamed "The Gray Lady,"[1] the *New York Times* newspaper had long been regarded within the industry as a national "newspaper of record".[2] The *Times* was founded as the *New-York Daily Times* on September 18, 1851, by banker George Jones and journalist and politician Henry Jarvis Raymond (1820–1869), then a Whig Party member and later second chairman of the newly organized Republican Party National Committee. Ironically, it was this conservative Republican-oriented journal—today the second largest newspaper in the United States behind the *Wall Street Journal*—that would play a pivotal role in American politics and change the nation forever.

By the 1970s, the *New York Times*, like most of the nation's newspapers, had been running articles about the progress of the war in Vietnam for more than a decade. At first, the articles were short informative pieces buried in the back of the paper, but as time went on and US involvement in the war grew, the fighting eventually became page-one headlines.

By 1971, after several failed political promises to bring the American troops home from the war, the fighting had grown more intense than ever. Numerous rounds of peace talks between the United States and North Vietnam had proved useless. It seemed as though US involvement in the war, which had originally been expected to last from six months to a year, would drag on forever. No one in the country knew exactly how America had gotten so deeply entangled in a war so many thousands of miles away. Worse still, no one seemed to know how to get the country out. Few Americans yet understood the behind-the-scenes role that their government had played in getting their nation into what was quickly becoming America's most unpopular war *ever*.

Then early in 1971, the *New York Times* received from an anonymous source a huge number of classified (secret for reasons of national security) memos that had been commissioned by the US Department of Defense, which is housed in the Pentagon building in Washington, DC. The memos came to be known as the "Pentagon Papers." The memos outlined for the first time America's involvement in the war in Vietnam. They revealed how President Johnson had secretly paved the way to use combat forces in Asia. They detailed how the president had avoided consulting Congress before committing both ground and air forces to the war. They even went so far as to explain how the

In this 1971 photo of the *New York Times* office, we see people looking at a proof sheet of one of the pages with the secret Pentagon report on Vietnam.

United States had secretly shifted US government funds toward the war effort.

An Unconstitutional War

These memos were especially surprising to the editors of the *New York Times*, because the declaration of war is a task guaranteed only to Congress. No one politician—not even the president—has the authority to decide on his or her own to wage war. That's a guarantee that the writers of the US Constitution built into the US Constitution in order to prevent a single tyrant—such as Germany's Adolf Hitler or Italy's Benito Mussolini prior to World War II—from gaining too much power and plunging the country into war. In failing to follow constitutional procedures and consulting with Congress before sending American troops to Vietnam, three American presidents—Kennedy, Johnson, and Nixon—failed in the proper execution of their presidential duties.

In May 1971, a group of the *New York Times'* editors decided that in the best interests of the United States the material in the Pentagon Papers had to be published. The American people and Congress had to be informed of the "secret war" that the US government had been waging in Vietnam. So on June 13, the newspaper published the first of a planned series of articles detailing some of the more than seven thousand pages of the report. The following day, the newspaper published a second installment. The articles detailed just how deceitful the US government had been.

Then on the evening of June 14, 1971, US Attorney General John N. Mitchell, at the request of President Nixon, sent a telegram to the *New York Times* requesting that the newspaper stop further publication of the articles based upon the Pentagon memos. Mitchell made his request on the grounds that such disclosures would cause "irreparable injury to the defense interests of the United States."[3]

In the telegram from Mitchell to the *New York Times'* president and publisher, Arthur Ochs Sulzberger, the attorney general said:

> I have been advised by the Secretary of Defense that the material published in the *New York Times* on June 13, 14, 1971, captioned "Key Texts from Pentagon's Vietnam Study" contains information relating to the national defense of the United States and bears a top secret classification.
>
> As such, publication of this information is directly prohibited by the provisions of the Espionage Law, Title 18, United States Code, Section 793.

Both Mitchell and Pentagon spokesman Jerry W. Friedheim cited sections of the Espionage and Censorship Chapter of the Federal criminal code. Section 793 of that code states:

> [W]hoever having unauthorized possession of, access to, or control over any document, writing, code book ... or information relating to the national defense which ... could be used to the injury of the United States or to the advantage of any foreign nation, willfully communicates, delivers, transmits ... the same to any person not entitled to receive it, or willfully retains the same and fails to deliver it to the officer or employee of the United States entitled to receive it ... shall be fined not more than $10,000 or imprisoned not more than ten years, or both.[4]

The Defense Department admitted that its attorneys did not know for sure if the *New York Times* was guilty of violating the security codes, or if the only guilty party was the person who had first provided the information to the paper. The confusion was caused in part because there was no precedent—no similar case in history to compare it to—in order to establish guilt or innocence. Nothing quite like this had ever happened before.

Following receipt of Mitchell's telegram, the *New York Times'* editors called an emergency meeting to discuss the issue. Within hours, they delivered a statement saying that the newspaper would "respectfully decline" the request of the attorney general. *Times'* personnel said they based their decision upon the belief that informing the American people of the material contained in the papers was in the people's best interests.[5] The next day, the newspaper published the third installment of its Pentagon Papers series.

An "Almost Incredible Deception"

Meanwhile, several senators and congressmen had read the *New York Times'* excerpts. Democratic Senator George S. McGovern of South Dakota, who had cosponsored a congressional measure to withdraw all American forces from Vietnam by the end of 1971, said the documents told

Nixon did not leave his presidency in the good graces of the American public. Though he was never impeached, he has even lower approval ratings than the two presidents who did face impeachment proceedings (they were not impeached)—Andrew Johnson and Bill Clinton.

a story of "almost incredible deception" toward Congress and the American people by the highest officials in government, including the president.[6] He went on to say that he could not see how any senator could ever again believe that it was safe to permit the executive branch (the president) to make foreign policy decisions without first consulting Congress.

Hugh Scott of Pennsylvania, the Republican Senate leader, said that the release of the documents was "a bad thing. It's a federal crime." Still, he described the contents of the secret papers as "very instructive and somewhat shocking."[7]

Representative Paul N. McCloskey, a Republican congressman from California, said the papers showed that "the issue of truthfulness in government is a problem as serious as that of ending the war itself." He went on to complain of "deceptive," "misleading," and "incomplete" briefings given to him during his recent visit to Southeast Asia, often while army officials who knew the statements to be untrue stood silent in his presence. "This deception is not a matter of protecting secret information from the enemy," McCloskey complained. "The intention is to conceal information from the people of the United States as if we were the enemy."[8]

In March 1971, a public poll reported that confidence in Nixon's handling of the war had dropped to 34 percent—the lowest approval rating in Nixon's presidency. A second survey showed that 51 percent of all Americans believed the conflict was "morally wrong."[9] Members of the House and the Senate were openly critical of Nixon and his war policies. On June 22, the Senate passed a nonbinding resolution calling for an end to the war and a complete withdrawal of all US troops. Nixon ignored the call.

On June 15, 1971, the US government filed a motion with the US District Court for the Southern District of New York requesting a temporary restraining order and an injunction against the *New York Times*. The temporary restraining order was designed to immediately stop the publication of the articles while the court took the time it needed to consider issuing an injunction, a court order, to prevent the newspaper from publishing the articles permanently. That same day, the court issued a temporary restraining order and a preliminary injunction, pending further review of the case.

It was a sweet—if temporary—victory for Nixon, who had had problems with the American press in the past and whose dislike of political reporters was well known. More importantly, the groundwork for legal struggle had been laid. Now the next move was up to the *New York Times*.

CHAPTER 3

A Case for the Government

A
ttorneys meeting to outline the *New York Times'*
case in favor of publishing the Pentagon Papers soon
envisioned a strategy they believed might win the day.
It involved the concept of "prior restraint," or the ability of
a government to halt publication of controversial or sensitive
information before it was ever published.

The basic concept of prior restraint in the United States
evolved from England, where John Locke and John Milton
argued strongly against the licensing schemes that limited
freedom of the press. Before the American Revolution,
prominent English legal commentator William Blackstone
had emphasized that freedom of the press essentially meant
freedom from prior restraint, but that subsequent remedies
remained available to punish abuses of that freedom after
publication. The idea was that prior restraints allowed the
government to stifle its critics, often based upon speculation,
assumptions, or political expediency. Prior restraints,

therefore, undermined liberty and the entire notion of freedom of the press.

No one knows exactly what the framers of the First Amendment to the US Constitution intended in order to protect the free speech and press clauses they held so dear, but most people who have studied the question agree that, at a minimum, the framers meant to make stifling the press via the use of prior restraints very difficult. At the same time, the most likely thought was that subsequent punishment for objectionable publications would be less problematic, because the statements at least would have been published so that US citizens would have the benefit of the viewing the controversial reports.

The government, on the other hand, believed it had a right to prevent the *New York Times* (and soon afterward the *Washington Post*) from publishing the Pentagon Papers. The newspapers disagreed and sought to invoke the prior-restraint doctrine in their defense.

At first glance, it appeared as if the newspapers had a very good argument. After all, in the 1931 case of *Near v. Minnesota*, the Supreme Court had taken a very strong line against prior restraints.

That case involved an attempt by a local prosecutor to shut down a newspaper that had harshly criticized local authorities as being corrupt. But Professor Alexander M. Bickel, whom the *New York Times* hired to lead its legal team, recognized that the *Near* case contained a national security exception to the rule against prior restraints. So, too, did the federal government.

The challenge was to figure out exactly what the "national security exception" meant.

Professor Bickel had to make a strategic decision. He could either argue for an almost absolute rule against prior restraints or contend that the government could not prevail under the unusual facts of the dispute. Bickel chose the latter alternative, and in doing so, he introduced a separation-of-powers theme— that Congress had not authorized the executive branch to enjoin the publication of material such as the Pentagon Papers and therefore the newspapers should prevail on a narrower (but perhaps less risky) legal theory than the absolute ban against prior restraints that many civil libertarians preferred.

As if the newspaper's job was not difficult enough, a new element entered the looming legal fray. And it would prove to play a major role in the pending battle.

Daniel Ellsberg

Daniel Ellsberg was born on April 7, 1931, in Chicago, Illinois. He graduated *summa cum laude* from Harvard University and the University of Cambridge. He served in the US Marine Corps and then, in 1959, joined the RAND Corporation—a research center (or "think tank") located in Santa Monica, California.

In 1964, Ellsberg was one of a select group of brilliant young scholars—the "whiz kids"—who had been recruited by Robert McNamara to work for the Pentagon. Ellsberg joined the US Department of Defense and the following year was sent to South Vietnam by the government. There he worked on

Daniel Ellsberg became an anti-war activist after his time in Vietnam. He decided to leak the Pentagon Papers to the press to help boost anti-war feelings in the country.

a special team whose mission was to locate and identify enemy spies. He did his job well.

But, in time, Ellsberg grew disillusioned by the progress of the war and returned to the United States. In 1967, he rejoined the RAND Corporation while remaining an active consultant to the US government on matters concerning the war in Vietnam. During this period, he helped to develop a secret study of the making of American policies concerning the war—the so-called "Pentagon Papers."

In 1970, Ellsberg left RAND to join in the anti-war movement protesting US involvement in Vietnam. The more Ellsberg protested, the more he came to believe just how immoral the war in Vietnam was. He began asking himself what he could do to help stop the war. Then an idea dawned on him.

Ellsberg decided to leak the information in the Pentagon Papers to the press. Once the American people learned of Washington's undercover operations, they would be furious. They would demand an end to the war—*immediately*.

When the *New York Times* released the first installment of the Pentagon Papers—copies of the documents and memos Ellsberg had retained from his years spent working with the government—President Nixon was furious. He immediately asked for an injunction demanding that the *Times* stop the publication of the documents. When the court refused, Nixon instructed his staff: "I want to know who is behind this and I want the most complete investigation that can be conducted. ... I don't want excuses. I want results. I want it done, whatever the costs."[1]

Kissinger, who had consulted briefly with Ellsberg shortly before Nixon had taken office, told Nixon that he had always considered Ellsberg a "fanatic" and a "drug abuser."[2] Attorney General John Mitchell said that Ellsberg was part of a Communist "conspiracy"[3] and suggested that he be tried for treason.

Nixon hastily called together a small group of loyal White House staff members, led by presidential assistant Egil "Bud" Krogh and lawyer David Young, to investigate Ellsberg's leak of classified documents to the press. The undercover investigative unit was soon dubbed the "plumbers" because of their task—to plug the "leaks" in the White House information pipeline. Nixon's special counsel, Charles Colson, enlisted other undercover operators, including Howard Hunt, who had once been with the CIA, and G. Gordon Liddy, a former Federal Bureau of Investigation (FBI) agent. Hunt and the other "plumbers" decided to break into the home of Lewis Fielding, Ellsberg's California-based psychiatrist. They hoped to find in Fielding's files enough information on Ellsberg to discredit him in the eyes of the public. The same group of "plumbers" later invaded the Democratic National Committee headquarters in the Watergate building in Washington, DC—an act that would eventually lead to Nixon's resignation.

The illegal activities of Ellsberg proved once and for all—to Nixon's satisfaction—that the leftists, liberals, Communists, and other opponents of the Vietnam War were dangerous anti-Americans who could not be trusted and had to be stopped. Krogh summarized the feelings of power at the White House best when he said, "Anyone who opposes us, we'll destroy. As a matter of fact, anyone who doesn't support us, we'll destroy."[4]

But by mid-1971, Nixon had failed to convince either the American public or the press of the danger that Ellsberg's activities had presented to the nation. Just the opposite, many Americans viewed Ellsberg as a national hero, someone who was willing to place his own integrity on the line in order to do whatever he could to unmask the years of deceit and secrecy in the government and to help bring a speedy end to the war.

Toward that end, Ellsberg enjoyed only limited success. His actions spurred Nixon and the US government to sue *New York Times* officials in an effort to force the newspaper to stop publishing the Pentagon Papers. But the war would continue for another two years before finally coming to a grudging halt with the signing of a peace agreement in Paris on January 27, 1973.

A Battle in the Courts

In the meantime, the *Times* found itself on the brink of battle. But this fight was not unfolding in a rice paddy halfway around the world; it was taking place in the courts. On June 15, 1971, the case of *New York Times Company v. United States* began. The US Justice Department, acting as the plaintiff—or the complaining party in the case—filed a motion seeking a temporary restraining order to prevent the *New York Times* from printing additional articles based upon the contents of the Pentagon Papers.

The suit was filed in the US District Court for the Southern District of New York, presided over by District Judge Murray I. Gurfein. The primary attorney for the government was J. Fred Buzhardt, general counsel for the Department of Defense.

Many others also worked on the case, including Attorney General John N. Mitchell, Assistant Attorney General Robert C. Mardian, and US Attorney for the Southern District of New York Whitney North Seymour.

The *New York Times*, in turn, enlisted the aid of Alexander Bickel, the professor at Yale Law School mentioned above, who was well known as a scholarly defender of the US Constitution. The *Times* also hired Floyd Abrams, a well-known practicing attorney from New York City, to represent the newspaper in its legal battle. Bickel argued against the government's request for a restraining order.

Meanwhile, the government insisted that the publication of the Pentagon Papers would jeopardize national security. There were classified documents in the newspaper's possession that could damage the ability of the United States to conduct its operations in the war in Vietnam. Some of the material might even prove harmful to US workers stationed in foreign countries around the world. The United States maintained a vast network of spies and counterspies to obtain much of the information that went into compiling the Pentagon Papers. Should the wrong people read the documents, they might be able to unmask the true identity of some of these undercover operatives, thus placing them in extreme danger.

So the US government wrote in its opening statement to the court:

This action has been commenced to preliminarily and permanently enjoin defendants and their agents from further disseminating documents consisting of forty-seven volumes entitled "History of U.S. Decision-Making Process on Vietnam Policy" [the Pentagon Papers]. Plaintiffs further seek to gain the recovery of the aforementioned documents from defendants. This memorandum is submitted in support of plaintiff's application for an Order temporarily restraining the defendants from further disseminating the aforementioned documents and requiring the delivery of the documents to this court pending the determination of plaintiff's motion for a preliminary injunction.[5]

The government specifically asked the court to order the return of the documents because, as of this time, it still had no idea of exactly what papers the *New York Times* officials had in their possession. The government's complaint continued:

Defendants are in possession of a forty-seven volume study entitled "History of United States Decision-Making Process on Vietnam Policy." This study is currently classified as "Top Secret—Sensitive" pursuant to the provision of Executive Order 10501. As defined in the Executive Order, top secret information is "that information or material, the defense aspect of which is paramount, and the unauthorized disclosure of which could result in exceptionally grave damage to the nation."

On June 13, 14, and 15, 1971, defendants published documents contained in the study. By telegram dated June 14, 1971, defendants were advised by the Attorney

General of the United States that further publication of the contents of the study will cause irreparable injury to the defense interests of the United States. In the telegram, defendants were requested to cease publication of the contents of the study and to return the study to the Department of Defense. Defendants have expressed the intention to continue to publish documents contained in the study until they are restrained from doing so by an Order of this Court.

Section 793(d) of Title 18 of the United States Code provides for criminal penalties against a person who, while lawfully in possession of information relating to the national defense which could be used to the injury of the United States, willfully communicates that information to persons not entitled to receive it or willfully fails to deliver it, on demand, to the officer of the United States entitled to receive it. The applicability of Section 793(d) has not been restricted to criminal actions.

Further publication of the contents of the study and defendants' continued refusal to return all of the papers to the Department of Defense will constitute a violation of Section 793(d). Moreover, such publication will result in irreparable injury to the interests of the United States, for which there is no adequate remedy at law. An injury is deemed irreparable when it cannot be adequately compensated in damages due to the nature of the injury itself or where there exists no pecuniary standard for the measurement of the damages. Irreparable injury also means "that species of damage, whether great or small, that ought not to be submitted to on the one hand or inflicted on the other."

In [this] case, defendants will suffer no injury if they cease to publish the contents of the study in their possession pending the determination of plaintiff's motion for a preliminary injunction. On the other hand, the national interest of the United States may be seriously damaged if the defendants continue to publish the contents of the study. Under circumstances in which no injury will result to defendants from the cessation of publication of the study in their possession and irreparable injury may result to the United States, the granting of a temporary restraining Order is appropriate. For the foregoing reasons, the plaintiff's application for a temporary restraining Order pending the determination of its motion for a preliminary injunction should be granted. Plaintiff's application for an Order temporarily restraining the further publication of the contents of the study in defendants' possession should be granted.[6]

After the request for a temporary restraining order was received by Judge Gurfein, he responded the same day by granting the government the temporary order, saying that any temporary harm done to the *New York Times* by the order "is far outweighed by the irreparable harm that could be done to the interests of the United States"[7] if the newspaper were allowed to continue publishing the secret reports while the courts further considered the matter. But the judge stopped short of ordering the newspaper to turn the Pentagon Papers over to the government. He stated:

> At this stage of the proceeding, I do not direct the *New York Times* or the other defendants to produce the documents pending the outcome of the litigation. I do not believe that the *New York Times* will willfully disregard the spirit of our restraining order. I am restraining the *New York Times* and the other defendants, however, from publishing or further disseminating or disclosing the documents ... pending the hearing of the Government's application for a preliminary injunction.
>
> The questions raised by this action [the Government's suit] are serious and fundamental. They involve not only matters of procedure, but matters of substance and ... of constitutional implication as well. ... I believe that the matter is so important and so involved with the history of the relationship between the security of the Government and a free press that a more thorough briefing than the parties have had an opportunity to do is required.[8]

In response to Gurfein's ruling, the *New York Times*—in a newspaper article published the next morning—agreed to comply. "*The Times* will comply with the restraining order issued by Judge Murray I. Gurfein. *The Times* will present its arguments against a permanent injunction at the hearing scheduled for Friday."[9]

The next day, Thursday, June 17, the government asked the court to order the *New York Times* to produce its copy of the Pentagon Papers for inspection and copying. Judge Gurfein declined, stating that he was not about to tolerate a governmental fishing expedition into the files of any newspaper. In response, the *New York Times* instead agreed to turn over for the government's inspection a list of descriptive headings for those memos in the newspaper's possession. That seemed to satisfy the government—for the time being, at least.

But the government was about to receive a surprise. On the morning of Friday, June 18, the *Washington Post* began publishing parts of the Pentagon Papers in a new series of articles. Now the government had not one, but two newspapers with which to deal. That same morning the hearing concerning a permanent injunction against the *New York Times* officials began in New York.

The *Times'* attorney, Bickel, quickly suggested that the hearing be dismissed because the case was moot—or did not merit a hearing—because the court's decision would have no practical effect on the actual controversy. Bickel based his request on the fact that, since another newspaper—the *Washington Post*—had already begun the publication of the Pentagon Papers, the same action by the *New York Times* was no longer of any consequence.

In support of his motion, Bickel had submitted to the court an affidavit—or sworn written statement—by James L. Greenfield, a *New York Times* editor. The affidavit stated that the *Washington Post's* news service had already begun

Neil Sheehan, who initially obtained the Pentagon Papers from Daniel Ellsberg, is shown on the far left here in this photo taken of the *New York Times* team, which included, left to right, A. M. Rosenthal and James L. Greenfield. The team won the Pulitzer Prize for publishing the Pentagon Papers.

distributing articles based upon the Pentagon Papers to its hundreds of newspaper subscribers throughout the country. Furthermore the Associated Press (AP), which by now had received its own copies of the articles based upon the Pentagon Papers, was busy distributing them to its 8,500 newspaper, television, and radio subscribers around the world. And this was only the tip of the iceberg!

Greenfield wrote in the affidavit:

It is evident that the very material which is the subject of the restraining order is receiving nationwide and worldwide dissemination from sources other than the *Times*. If the restraining order continue[s] in effect, the *Times* will suffer irreparable pecuniary [financial] and professional damage in that once the documents are published ... they will lose their newsworthy value to the *Times* as an exclusive story and will cause the *Times* to lose all benefit from the large sums of money, time and energy expended by the *Times* in compiling this story. In fact, if the order continues in effect, the *Times* alone will be restrained from publishing its own carefully compiled story.[10]

The government's lawyers, US Attorney Whitney North Seymour and Assistant US Attorney Michael D. Hess, insisted that the case against the *Times* was still valid—despite the publication of the Pentagon Papers by the *Washington Post* and other newspapers:

Your Honor, I am informed that Mr. Robert Mardian, who is the Assistant Attorney General of the United States in charge of the National Security Division, is here in court and he has informed us that these articles in the *Washington Post* will be reviewed by the Justice Department and action will be taken [against the *Post*] if it appears to be necessary.[11]

And, true enough, while the hearing was unfolding in New York, the government, concerned about the *Washington Post's* publication of the Pentagon Papers, brought legal action against *that* newspaper before Judge Gerhard A. Gesell in the District Court of the District of Columbia. Gesell subsequently denied the government's request for a temporary restraining order, and that evening, the government appealed Gesell's decision. The Court of Appeals for the DC Circuit overturned Gesell and granted the government's request for a temporary restraining order by a 2–1 vote.

Meanwhile, Hess continued to argue the main thrust of the government's case against the *New York Times*. He argued that by publishing the Pentagon Papers, the *Times* was violating the national security interests of the United States, and by doing so, was guilty of a violation of law and required to cease all such publishing. It was a matter of national interest, Hess argued—pure and simple—and it superseded any right of the press to publish. Executive Order 10501, dealing with matters of national security and the need for secrecy, spelled that out.

Next, Whitney North Seymour, who had received permission from the court to share the oral argument on behalf of the government, addressed the bench:

> May it please the Court, as we see it, the issue in this proceeding is a very simple one, and that is whether, when an unauthorized person comes into possession of documents which have been classified under lawful procedures, that

person may unilaterally declassify those documents in his sole discretion.

The position of the Government in the proceeding is equally simple. These are stolen documents. They are classified. They compromise our current military and defense plans and intelligence operations and jeopardize our international relations.

Contrary to some of the suggestions in counsel's argument [in the *New York Times'* defense], and in the brief, that what this amounts to is a bald attempt at suppression and censorship, we have attempted to approach the matter with the highest regard for the constitutional rights of all concerned and in an orderly, lawful process. ...

We are now at the point where we are presenting the matter on the merits, and I think it is important to recognize at the outset that our sole purpose here is to present the evidence to the Court so that the matter can be decided impartially and objectively on the facts and on the merits and in accordance with the law.[12]

Following Seymour's opening statement, the government went on to introduce various witnesses in support of its contention that the Pentagon Papers were highly sensitive military reports that needed to be classified. Seymour also reviewed with the witnesses the process for declassifying documents—that is, taking secret documents and downgrading their classification until they are available for review by the general public.

Dennis James Doolin, a witness for the government, relayed the process by which a document is declassified:

> When either a declassification takes place or a downgrading in the classification takes place, a notice is sent to the original addresses, say, if it is a cable, for example, that is later downgraded, they are notified and the classification is changed on the document.
>
> Other documents are downgraded at the end of set calendar periods, three years, for example. Certain documents are downgraded until they become unclassified. So there is an established procedure and there are officers, for example, in the Department of State, in the office of the Secretary of Defense, in each of the military departments, the services, as well as the Joint Chiefs of Staff, there are historians and people to assist researchers, scholars on matters of this type.[13]

Seymour went on to ask if there might not be numerous documents within the Pentagon Papers that were classified as top secret, and Doolin agreed that there were. Then he added that some of them were among the documents that the *New York Times* had not yet published but intended to do so, with the court's permission.

Next the government called as a witness Admiral Francis J. Blouin of the US Navy. Blouin, asked to comment about a particular article among the secret papers that the *New York Times* planned to publish, replied,

Well, I can say in open session here that there is a summary in that report which describes what happens, but then it goes on and gets into very intimate details on the command organization of the United States, and I feel that to go any farther in describing that or the forces involved and how they are generated is very definitely damaging to the best interests of the United States.[14]

Finally, the government called William Butts Macomber, the Deputy Undersecretary of State for Administration in the Department of State, to the stand. Seymour asked him if, in his opinion, the publication of portions of the Pentagon Papers had already jeopardized international relations. Macomber replied:

A historic and present absolute essential to the conduct of diplomacy is the capacity for governments to be able to deal in confidence with each other and to have confidence that when they are dealing in confidence, that confidence will not be violated.

If governments cannot deal that way ... the communication which is the lifeblood of diplomacy is cut off and in fact diplomacy is crippled very severely.

This not only damages the capacity for the United States to pursue its security interests ... but it damages the prospects that all nations seek to develop an enduring and just peace in the world.

If we cannot communicate privately with each other, the diplomatic process, which is the best hope we have to achieve this just and lasting peace, will be denied not only to this country but to others.[15]

Seymour then asked Macomber if he thought that disclosing some of the material within the Pentagon Papers might have any impact on diplomatic relations or treaty discussions with foreign governments.

"Yes, sir," Macomber replied, "It would have an adverse impact."[16]

At that point, the government rested its case. Seymour sat down, secure in the knowledge that he had done a reasonably good job in presenting the government's case.

And to outsiders viewing the hearing, he would have been right. But one thing was certain: the *New York Times* would have to go to some lengths to refute the expert testimony the government had presented. The big question facing them was could the *Times* do it?

CHAPTER 4
The *New York Times* Responds

A s soon as the attorneys for the *New York Times* had been notified on June 15 that the government might sue the paper to stop publication of the Pentagon Papers, they began mapping out their strategy. The basis for the newspaper's defense was one of the most basic and sacred concepts in American law. It was the First Amendment to the US Constitution, which states: "Congress shall make no law respecting an establishment or religion, or prohibiting the free exercise thereof; or abridging the freedom of speech or of the press; or the right of the people peaceably to assemble, and to petition the Government for a redress of grievances."

By asking the court to issue an injunction prohibiting the *New York Times'* publication of the Pentagon Papers, the government was in violation of one of the most basic principles of the First Amendment—freedom of the press.

The newspaper's attorneys also intended to argue the point that just because the government claims that some

These are the lawyers representing the *Times*. From left, in foreground, Lawrence McKay, William Hegarty, and James Goodale, *Times'* vice president. In rear, from left, Alexander Bickel and Floyd Abrams (with briefcase).

material is top secret, it is not necessarily so. There had been many cases over the years in which material marked "classified" had actually been kept from the public, not because releasing it might jeopardize national security, but because doing so might embarrass the government or make it look bad in the eyes of other governments and the American voters.

So on June 18, 1971, when the *Times'* attorneys, Floyd Abrams, William E. Hegarty, Alexander Bickel, and Lawrence J. McKay, entered the US District Court of New York, they were prepared to deal with the government's arguments concerning the newspaper's tampering with classified material.

When Judge Gurfein made a comment in his opening remarks about the possibility that the *New York Times'* publication of the Pentagon Papers might result in a foreign government breaking some secret military code, Bickel replied:

> Your Honor, if it is true, it is true then dealing with historical documents going back even forty years, fifteen, ten. Every newspaper has to be concerned whether it is going to break a code then, your Honor. ... It is common knowledge that the security of codes is insured by their being changed with extreme rapidity in very short order ... there is nothing in there [the Pentagon Papers] less than three years old. To think that a document like that could possibly compromise a code is within my understanding and within the understanding of everybody at *The Times*, within the kind of common knowledge that anybody can be expected to have and that must govern the work of a newspaper.[1]

In response to Judge Gurfein's comment that he wished the *New York Times* and the government had simply gotten together and discussed the matter prior to the newspaper having published the documents, Bickel said:

There are two reasons for that, your Honor, which I hope will commend themselves to you.

One reason we see is that it is utterly inconsistent with the First Amendment on any matters except with the rare exception of wartime activities when it is clear to everyone that the citizen, as such, cannot have a judgment that is reliable, or in … national crises, as during the Cuban missile crisis, when it is again evident on its face of things that the judgment, the news judgment of a newspaper, may get into dangerous areas.

With those exceptions, we cannot submit what we are going to print in a newspaper … to government approval.[2]

Bickel, within a few short moments, had struck at the very heart of the government's suit. The material contained in the Pentagon Papers did not relate to a national crisis, and it was not being published during time of war—not officially, at least. So how could it be considered sensitive? Even though the United States was deeply involved in the ongoing conflict in Vietnam, war between the United States and North Vietnam had never been *officially* declared.

Then just as quickly, Bickel moved into another area of defense—that of exactly what material the government has a right to classify:

I am not claiming, for example, if in time of war or national emergency a troopship leaves New York Harbor and the *New York Times* takes it into its head to publish the date of departure and the date of arrival and the probable course, thus leading to the destruction of that ship, that is protected by the First Amendment. ... But, your Honor, as applied to this case, as applied to the materials that have been published, to the materials that it was made clear we still have ... the application to censor us on the circumstances of this case, on the grounds that the Government is discomfited and anything that discomfits the Government because it may be put in an unfavorable light with a foreign government as a result of internal political discussion— any application of censorship to us on that ground, which is how we view the case, is a flagrant violation of the First Amendment, in our view.[3]

From this point, Bickel and Hegarty cross-examined the government's witnesses, concentrating on the areas they stressed earlier. Then Bickel made his concluding remarks, and within a matter of a few hours, the case had been argued. Judge Gurfein suggested that the attorneys contact him at 11 a.m. the following day to see if he had yet reached a verdict.

The Judge Decides

The following morning, the attorneys did call Judge Gurfein. Yes, he told them, he had reached a decision. So on Saturday, June 19, Gurfein denied the government's motion for an injunction against the *New York Times*. But, still concerned about the damage that might be done to the government if the

Pentagon Papers were published while the continuing legal action worked its way through the courts, Gurfein added, "The temporary restraining order will continue, however, until such time during the day as the Government may seek a stay from a Judge of the Court of Appeals for the Second Circuit."[4]

So, while the newspaper won its first-round bid to prevent the government from receiving an injunction, it lost its attempt to have the temporary restraining order lifted. In effect, the *New York Times* had won, but it still could not publish any more of the series that it had broken to the American public.

The Government Appeals

Within minutes of Judge Gurfein's decision, the attorneys for the government appealed the case to Judge Irving R. Kaufman of the Second Circuit Court of Appeals. Judge Kaufman, after reading the government's argument, granted a stay—or a postponement—of the lower court's decision until June 21.

On Monday, June 21, a three-judge panel of the court of appeals met to hear the appeal by the government. The court decided to continue the stay until the following day, Tuesday, June 22, so that the full Second Circuit Court could review the case.

On June 22, Whitney North Seymour and Michael D. Hess argued the government's case for an injunction in the Second Circuit Court in New York before an eight-judge panel headed by Chief Judge Henry J. Friendly. At the same time, the attorneys for the *New York Times*—the same attorneys who had represented the newspaper in the lower court—made a motion before the appeals court to overturn the temporary restraining order so that the newspaper could resume publishing its series while the case was being heard.

At 5 p.m. on June 23, the Court of Appeals for the Second Circuit Court met to consider the case and, in a 5–3 decision, voted to send the case back to Judge Gurfein for further hearing, in light of additional evidence that the government had supplied to the court.

It also upheld the temporary restraining order against the newspaper.

So while the government had not yet won its case, it had at least accomplished one of its goals—preventing the *New York Times* from publishing any additional Pentagon Papers articles while the matter continued winding its way through the courts.

Taking the Case to the Supreme Court

The following day, June 24, the attorneys for the *Times* filed a petition for a writ of certiorari, a request that would take their case against the government to the highest court—the US Supreme Court. They also requested permission to present an oral argument of the case before the Supreme Court and filed an application for vacatur of stay, requesting that the Court overturn the temporary restraining order upheld by the appeals court.

In its application for certiorari, *Times'* attorney William Hegarty attempted to convince the Supreme Court that the newspaper's publication of the Pentagon Papers should not be restrained, because by this time a number of other newspapers had begun publishing articles based upon the documents. By being restrained from doing likewise, the *New York Times* was being unfairly singled out and would suffer both loss of prestige and income. Among the written remarks Hegarty sent to John Marshall Harlan, associate justice of the Supreme Court, were the following:

> The district court denied the preliminary injunction after a hearing. By affidavits and the testimony of witnesses at the hearing, the Government tried to demonstrate that the publication of the material in question [the Pentagon Papers] should be restrained because it would gravely prejudice [or harm] the defense interests of the United States or result in irreparable injury to the United States. The district court found that the Government failed to sustain its burden [of proof]. Specifically, the district court directed the Government to present any document from the "History," the disclosure of which in the Government's judgment would irreparably harm the United States. The Government's affidavits and testimony ... discussed several of the documents. The district court found either that disclosure of those specific documents would not be harmful [to the Government] or that any harm resulting from disclosure would be insufficient to override First Amendment interests. ...

As a result of the decision of the Court of Appeals for the Second Circuit, the petitioner [the *Times*] continues to be enjoined [prevented] from publishing the historical documents and articles it seeks to print, and this prior restraint [restraining order] will continue for additional significant periods of time. A number of newspapers and news wire services have already published news stories which petitioner has been enjoined from printing. It is reasonable to expect that other publications will follow. The documents themselves have rapidly become increasingly public and unless immediate relief is granted and the petitioner is permitted to freely publish—as the District Court ordered—it will suffer irremediable harm. News no longer current is stale and of severely diminished intrinsic value.[5]

Toward the end of the eleven-page document, Hegarty went on to request that the Court promptly consider hearing oral arguments in the case, since the very timeliness of the materials the *New York Times* was seeking to publish and the seriousness of the matter at stake—freedom of the press— were crucial to the best interests of the citizens of the United States.

Following Hegarty's application for certiorari to the Supreme Court, the government responded with a request for certiorari of its own—this one against the *Washington Post*—along with a written memo opposing the *New York Times'* request that the Court overturn the temporary restraining order.

On Friday, June 25, 1971, the US Supreme Court issued an order granting a petition for certiorari to the *New York Times* and setting the oral arguments for the following morning. The Court went on to state:

> The restraint imposed upon the *New York Times* by the Court of Appeals for the Second Circuit is continued, pending argument and decision in this case. For purposes of argument, this case is consolidated with *United States v. The Washington Post*, petition for certiorari this day granted.[6]

Four justices—Hugo Black, William Douglas, William Brennan, and Thurgood Marshall—voted to have the temporary restraining order against the *New York Times* lifted and the case returned to the lower courts, but they were overruled by the majority.

So, in the end, the *New York Times* won half its battle. It had succeeded in having the US Supreme Court agree to hear the case, even though the Court, by a split decision, voted to continue the restraining order.

Now all that was left for the *Times* was the hard part. Next on the newspaper's agenda: presenting its case to the highest court in the land.

CHAPTER 5

Before the Supreme Court

Anxious to prove once and for all that the government had no right to suppress news or censor information except during time of war or national emergency, the *Times* looked forward to making their arguments before the Supreme Court. On the other hand, the government, convinced that it was on solid ground in restricting the publication of information detrimental to national security, was equally anxious to appear before the Court.

But the government had another even more compelling reason for wanting to take the case to the Supreme Court. In the case of the *United States v. Washington Post*—the nearly identical case unfolding at the same time as the *New York Times* case—the results had been anything but identical to that of the *Times'* case.

The initial courtroom appearances of both newspapers had ended similarly. Judge Gurfein had ruled in New York against the government. Judge Gesell had done likewise in Washington, DC.

The justices sitting on the US Supreme Court during the *New York Times v. United States* case were, seated from left to right, Associate Justices John M. Harlan and Hugo Black; Chief Justice Warren E. Burger; Associate Justices William O. Douglas and William Brennan, and standing from left, Associate Justices Thurgood Marshall, Potter Stewart, Byron R. White, and Harry A. Blackmun.

The government then took both cases to the appeals court. The court in New York ruled *against* the *New York Times*, sending the case back to the lower court, and continuing the restraining order. But the court in DC ruled in favor of the *Washington Post*, lifting the restraining order and allowing the *Post* to resume publication of the documents.

If the government did not move quickly to argue its case against *both* newspapers, it might be too late. With dozens—or perhaps even hundreds—of newspapers planning on beginning their own Pentagon Papers series soon, the government needed to have the highest court in the land place an injunction against the release of the documents. Once that occurred, it would be relatively simple to get all the other newspapers to stop publishing the series.

Much to the government's delight, once the Supreme Court had agreed to hear oral arguments in the case, the Court imposed identical restrictions on the *Washington Post* and the *New York Times*. Neither newspaper was allowed to publish Pentagon Papers material that the government had included in a list it had earlier furnished the Court. The list contained items that the government considered "dangerous." Although the Court order allowed the two newspapers to publish any Pentagon Papers material *not* on the government's list, both newspapers declined. Newspaper personnel said that "printing an article whose content was dictated by government officials would amount to submitting to censorship,"[1] and that, they felt, was contrary to their First Amendment rights.

An Important Case

Meanwhile, the Supreme Court acknowledged the importance of the *New York Times'* case by scheduling a rare Saturday session to hear the arguments. On the morning of June 26, attorneys for the government, including Solicitor General Erwin N. Griswold, who had served as dean of Harvard Law School for twenty years before becoming a member of the government's staff, joined *Times'* attorney Alexander Bickel and the *Washington Post's* attorney William R. Glendon. They met inside the main chambers of the US Supreme Court building in Washington, DC, to argue their cases. As solicitor general, Griswold's job included leading the government's appeals' team in the Supreme Court and, at times, in lower courts.

Griswold stated:

It is important, I think, to get this case in perspective. The case, of course, raises important and difficult problems about the Constitutional right of free speech and of the free press. We have heard much about that from the press in the last two weeks. But it also raises important questions of the equally fundamental and important right of the government to function. Great emphasis has been put on the First Amendment, and rightly so, but there is also involved here a fundamental question of separation of powers in the sense of the power and authority which the Constitution allocates to the President as chief executive and as Commander-in-Chief of the Army and Navy.

Involved in that there is also the question of the integrity of the institution of the Presidency, whether that institution, one of the three great powers under the separation of powers, can function effectively.[2]

Then Justice Stewart commented to the solicitor general, "Your case depends upon the claim, as I understand it, that the disclosure of this information would result in an immediate grave threat to the security of the United States of America."

The solicitor general replied, "Yes, Mr. Justice."

Stewart continued, "However it [the information] was acquired, and however it was classified."

"Yes, Mr. Justice," Griswold agreed, "but I think the fact that it was obviously acquired improperly is not irrelevant in the consideration of that question. I repeat, obviously acquired improperly."[3]

After some bantering back and forth about whether or not the government would consider declassifying parts of the Pentagon Papers in the event that it won its case, Justice Stewart returned to his earlier questioning.

"Mr. Solicitor General … this brings me back to my original question of a few moments ago as to what the real basic issue in this case is. As I understand it, you are not claiming that you are entitled to an injunction simply or solely because this is classified material."

"No," replied Griswold. Then Justice Stewart and Griswold continued:

Stewart: Nor do I understand it that you are claiming that you are entitled to an injunction because it was stolen from you, that it is your property. You are claiming rather and basically that whether or not it is classified or however it is classified, and however it was acquired by these newspapers, the public disclosure of this material would pose a grave and immediate danger to the security of the United States of America, period.

Griswold: Yes, Mr. Justice.

Stewart: Now, isn't that correct?

Griswold: Yes, Mr. Justice.[4]

Griswold then went on to present the argument that, in his opinion, the Supreme Court should uphold the Second Circuit Court of Appeals' verdict and return the *New York Times* case to the lower court for further hearings. Griswold summed up his argument by talking once again about the grave danger in which the United States had been placed by the publication of some of the Pentagon Papers.

The government had presented its case for nearly an hour.

Bickel Responds

Following the government's opening arguments, Bickel addressed the Court on behalf of the *Times*. He pointed out that although the *Times* began publishing the Pentagon Papers on the morning of June 13, it did not hear from the government until the evening of June 15—a full thirty-six hours after the paper ran its first installment. Just how sensitive could the materials have been, Bickel commented, if it took the government a day and a half to respond to them and another day to get a court-ordered restraining order against the *Times*?

Furthermore, Bickel argued, Judge Gurfein, in looking for specific documents of the gravest importance to the nation's welfare, failed to find any.

Erwin Griswold was appointed solicitor general in 1967. The solicitor general's job is to argue for the United States in cases that come before the Supreme Court.

The record will clearly show that the judge's sole purpose ... and continuously expressed intent was to provoke from the Government witnesses something specific, to achieve from them the degree of guidance that he felt he needed in order to penetrate this enormous record. It is our judgment, and it was his, that he got very little, perhaps almost nothing. ... I think the Government gave Judge Gurfein all it had.[5]

Bickel went on to summarize the *New York Times'* defense "on principles, as we view them, of the separation of powers, which we believe deny the existence of inherent Presidential authority on which an injunction can be based."[6]

Bickel continued, saying that he doubted the president's authority extended so far as to be able to impose prior restraint upon the free press except in times of war or national emergency. The rule against prior restraint prohibits government from banning expression of ideas prior to their publication.

As Chief Justice Hughes formulated it [in the case of *Near v. Minnesota*] it referred to—actually it said—we would all assume that a prior restraint might be possible to prevent actual obstruction of the recruiting service, and this is the Chief Justice's language, or the publication of sailing dates of transport [ships], or the number and location of troops. I suppose that ... on the sailing dates of ships and the location of troops, there is a very specific statute. It is 18 U.S.C. 794, which has not been cited against us, which is inapplicable, which is why it has not been cited against us, because that is not what we report. That is not in our paper. ...

Whatever that case may be, it cannot be this case ... there is no applicable statute under which we [the *New York Times*] are covered.[7]

Justice Stewart then broke into the conversation and said to Bickel, "Your standard [for deciding which material is too sensitive to publish] is that it has to be an extremely grave event to the nation and it has to be directly proximately caused by the publication."

"That is correct," Bickel replied.[8]

After several more minutes of questions and answers between the justices and the attorney, Bickel concluded his arguments. Then William R. Glendon, the attorney representing the interests of the *Washington Post*, addressed the bench.

The *Post* Weighs In

Glendon told of how both the New York and Washington lower court cases had gone, how both Judge Gurfein in New York and Judge Gesell in Washington had failed to grant the government an injunction against either the *New York Times* or the *Washington Post* because the government was not able to convince either court of the immediate and grave danger posed by the publication of the Pentagon Papers. That was because, Glendon insisted, there were no dangerous secrets contained in the Pentagon Papers.

Chief Justice Warren Burger then inquired,

Can anyone know in any certain sense the consequences of disclosure of sources of information—for example, the upsetting of negotiations ... in Paris [the Vietnam War peace talks] or possible negotiations that we don't know anything about in the release of war prisoners and that sort of thing?

Glendon replied:

Your Honor, I think if we are going to place possibilities or conjecture against suspension or abridgement of the First Amendment, the answer is obvious. ... All that we have [in this case] does not justify suspending the First Amendment. Yet that is what has happened here. ... Judge Gurfein used the words up in New York, and I am sure used them respectfully, but he said when there is a security breach, people get the jitters. I think maybe the Government has a case of the jitters here. But that, I submit, does not warrant the stopping [of] the press on this matter.[9]

Glendon continued this line of argument for nearly fifteen minutes until Chief Justice Burger commented that some of the Pentagon documents, classified in 1965, might no longer be subject to classification.

"That is correct, Your Honor, and furthermore, some of these documents which were classified go back to 1945. The documents are that ancient."[10]

Then Glendon struck at a particularly relevant point in the case—the government's insistence that the newspapers had illegally obtained the documents that were now in their possession, and by doing so were guilty of committing a crime:

[T]he Government and the press ... are naturally in opposite corners—the press is trying to get as much news as it can and the Government, particularly where it may be embarrassing or where [the Government] may be overly concerned or may feel [the news] is embarrassing or may, in Judge Gurfein's words, have the jitters, [the Government] is trying to prevent that sometimes. On other occasions, the Government engages itself in leaks, because some official will feel that in the public interest it is well for the public to know, and that overrides any particular judgment of security or classification.[11]

In short, Glendon had brought before the Court a strategy that had been used by Washington politicians for years. Whenever a sensitive story needed to be told—such as the story of allowing homosexuals to serve in the military or raising taxes on America's middle-class families—a president would often "leak" the story to the press. If the American people were strongly against the issue, the president would deny that it had been his idea. If the people were in favor of it, the president would step forward to claim the glory.

For many years, Washington had used this "double-standard" game of cat and mouse with the press. Now suddenly, the government was claiming that, because the Pentagon Papers had not come from official government sources, they had been obtained illegally.

Glendon continued:

The record, Your Honors, will find is [filled] with instances where leaks of confidential, secret, and top-secret material have been given to the press, or the press has found them out and published them, and of course nothing has happened. I think that is significant because this is the sort of thing we feel we are talking about.[12]

So the *New York Times* and the *Washington Post* concluded their oral arguments.

Following the petitioner's arguments, Solicitor General Griswold was granted a period of time for rebuttal, or the opportunity to respond to his opponent's arguments. In his rebuttal, he argued that, although there were few—and possibly no—cases of prior restraint against the press in the past, one was merited in this case. The sensitive nature of the material, he argued, made that clear.

When Justice Stewart commented that prior restraint of publication by a newspaper was unconstitutional, Griswold admitted, "It is a very serious matter. There is no doubt about it, and so is the security of the United States a very serious matter."[13]

By the time Griswold had concluded his rebuttal, the justices were satisfied that they had heard everything they needed to hear. So the Court adjourned, after which the justices met to discuss the case until 6 p.m.

Meanwhile, the Court's final meeting for the 1970–1971 term was scheduled for Monday, June 28. If the Court was going to issue an opinion during this term, it would have to act quickly. And so it did.

CHAPTER 6

A Quick Decision

When Monday arrived, an anxious nation awaited the Supreme Court's decision. When the decision failed to come—and failed to come on Tuesday as well—some people began to speculate as to what was happening. During its arguments, the government had asked the Supreme Court to return the case to the lower courts for further hearings and to adopt a standard that would halt any publication of the material if "it will affect lives, it will affect the termination of the [Vietnam] war, it will affect the progress of recovering our prisoners of war."[1]

Could the Court, people began to wonder, be considering doing just that? Is that what was causing the delay? Finally, on Wednesday, June 30, the Supreme Court met in a hastily called special session. At 2:30 p.m. in a hushed courtroom, Chief Justice Warren E. Burger read the Court's decision. In a 6–3 split vote, the justices found as follows:

We granted certiorari … in these cases in which the United States seeks to enjoin the *New York Times* and the *Washington Post* from publishing the contents of a classified study entitled "History of US Decision-Making Process on Vietnam Policy."

Any system of prior restraints of expression comes to this Court bearing a heavy presumption against its constitutional validity. … The Government thus carries a heavy burden of showing justification for the imposition of such a restraint. … The District Court for the Southern District of New York in the *New York Times* case and the District Court for the District of Columbia and the Court of Appeals for the District of Columbia Circuit in the *Washington Post* case held that the Government had not met that burden. We agree.[2]

So the Supreme Court, in a monumental 6–3 split decision, voted to reject the government's appeal for a permanent injunction against the *New York Times* and the *Washington Post* and lifted the restraining orders against the newspapers.

The Dissenting Opinions

Among the dissenters was the chief justice who, along with associate justices Harry A. Blackmun and John M. Harlan, defended their decision based upon the belief that the president had the unrestrained authority to prevent confidential materials affecting foreign policy from being published in the press. Furthermore they felt that the "frenzied train of events"[3] in the cases had not given the lower courts enough time to consider the case, and they voted to retain the restraints against the newspapers while sending the case back to the lower courts for additional hearings.

The Concurring Opinions

The six justices who voted in favor of the newspapers broke down into two groups of three. The first group of justices—William Douglas, Hugo Black, and Thurgood Marshall—held the "absolutist" view. They believed that the press may not be suppressed under any circumstances—no matter what the threat to national security might be.

The second group—Potter Stewart, Byron White, and William Brennan—held the more common view that the press could be prevented from publishing only in the event of war or time of national emergency. They agreed that no such threat existed with the publication of the Pentagon Papers.[4]

In a clear reference to what he saw as the government's shady handling of the war in Vietnam, Justice Black stated in his opinion that publications such as the *New York Times'* and the *Washington Post's* were exactly what the First Amendment was designed to protect:

> Paramount among the responsibilities of a free press is the
> duty to prevent any part of the government from deceiving
> the people and sending them off to distant lands to die of
> foreign fevers and foreign shot and shell.

In my view, far from deserving condemnation for their courageous reporting, the *New York Times* and the *Washington Post* and the other newspapers should be commended for serving the purpose that the Founding Fathers saw so clearly. In revealing the workings of Government that led to the Vietnam War, the newspapers nobly did precisely that which the founders hoped and trusted they would do.[5]

Justice Douglas, in agreeing with Justice Black, said that the First Amendment's purpose is to prevent "governmental suppression of embarrassing information" and that the cases "constitute a flouting of the principles of the First Amendment."[6]

Justice Brennan, commenting on the temporary restraining order issued against the newspapers, said that the orders should not have been imposed because the government had referred to security problems that might occur only in the most general of terms.

Justice Stewart, in the concluding remarks of his opinion, said simply,

I cannot say that disclosure of any of [the documents] will surely result in direct, immediate, and irreparable damage to our Nation or its people. That being so, there can under the First Amendment be but one judicial resolution of the issues before us.[7]

Justice White, in concurring with the Court majority, likewise spent considerable time talking about the government's failure to show that the Pentagon Papers contained material that might be seriously damaging to the nation, while Justice Marshall addressed the question of the separation of powers:

> The Constitution provides that Congress shall make laws, the President execute laws, and courts interpret laws. ... It did not provide for government by injunction in which the courts and the Executive can "make law" without regard to the action of Congress. ... [I]t is clear that Congress has specifically rejected passing legislation that would have clearly given the President the power he seeks here and made the current activity of the newspapers unlawful. When Congress specifically declines to make conduct unlawful, it is not for this Court to re-decide those issues— to overrule Congress.[8]

Meanwhile, Arthur Ochs Sulzberger, the president and publisher of the *New York Times*, said at a news conference held in New York that he "never really doubted that this day would come and that we'd win." His reaction was "complete joy and delight."[9]

On the other hand, US Solicitor General Griswold was quoted as saying, "Maybe the newspapers will show a little restraint in the future."[10]

But the truth was closer to how Alexander Bickel, the Yale law professor who had argued the case for the *New York Times*, saw it. Bickel said in a telephone conversation with the newspaper that the ruling placed the press in a "stronger position"[11] and that in the future no Federal District Court judge would issue a restraining order against a newspaper

Arthur Ochs Sulzberger became the publisher of the *New York Times* in 1963.

merely on the government's dissatisfaction with the paper's publication of a particular story.

So the first case ever in which a temporary restraining order was issued against a newspaper in the interest of "national security" had finally had its day in court. The outcome could not help but strengthen the First Amendment protections of freedom of the press.

CHAPTER 7
A Free Press

Censorship of the press has existed for much longer than the United States. As early as AD 1515, the Roman Catholic Church decreed at the Council of the Lateran that no publication could be issued anywhere the Church had jurisdiction without first obtaining the written permission of the bishop or of the inquisitor of the diocese. Before long, the notion of censoring the press was widely accepted, and many civil governments throughout Europe adopted the policy. Some countries still censor their national presses.

In England, the press fought long and hard over the years until, today, it enjoys nearly total liberty—at least during times of peace. During wartime, though, strict censorship is imposed over the British press.

America's Founding Fathers, hard at work drafting a new set of laws for an awakening nation, were well aware of the problems that the lack of a free press had caused in Europe. When the first ten amendments—called the Bill of Rights—were added to the

©1971 HERBLOCK

This political cartoon shows Richard Nixon as one of the handles on a pair of scissors with "Attempted Censorship" etched on one of the blades.

original seven articles of the US Constitution, freedom of the press was high on the list. The Constitution's framers knew from bitter experience that censorship of the press often led to government corruption. They realized that the best way to keep political corruption from happening in America was to keep the press free from governmental influence.

For more than two centuries, US courts have jealously guarded the freedoms guaranteed within the First Amendment. The case for the *New York Times*, in the eyes of most working journalists, could not have ended differently. If the Court had decided against the *New York Times* and prevented it from publishing the Pentagon Papers—or even forced the newspaper to clear parts of the series with the government before publishing—the values of a free press in America would have been seriously jeopardized.

Freedom of the press does not mean that the government cannot withhold—or attempt to withhold—information from the press. Indeed, the government does so frequently, often on a daily basis. In that regard, it has as much right to do so as any individual.

But neither does freedom of the press mean that the government can prevent the press from publishing news once the press has obtained the necessary information and means to do so.

A Sad Example

Unfortunately, freedom of the press has not been high on every world leader's list of democratic freedoms. During the late 1930s and early 1940s, the idea of a democratic republic, very much like the one we have here in the United States, preventing the press from freely publishing information on the workings of the government, was unheard of. Yet during those ten years in history, the free press became anything *but* free.

Led by a man who had been defeated for the office of president before finally filling that position in 1934, the government worked long and hard to conceal information from the press that would prove embarrassing or damaging to the government.

In time, that leader succeeded in turning the press into just one more arm of his administration. Soon the press was printing only the information that had first been cleared with the government, giving that government a free hand to run the country as it wished without the citizens learning of the corruption, vice, and hysteria that were slowly sweeping the government. By the time this man's administration had been forced from power, millions of people had been killed, their homes destroyed, their property seized. And one of the bloodiest eras in world history had come to a sad and bitter end.

These events occurred in Nazi Germany. The leader was Adolf Hitler. And the world, some half a century later, is still struggling to recover. Some people say that such a tragedy could never happen in America. Others believe that one of the only things preventing this tragedy from happening in America is a free press.

CHAPTER 8

A Far-Reaching Concept

Freedom of the press—it is a strange-sounding phrase anchoring an even stranger-sounding concept: a press uninfluenced by outside political forces.

But what exactly is freedom of the press? Where did the concept come from? And how important is it to the functioning of a democratic society such as the United States of America? The answers to these questions may be important to understanding just how critical a role the 1971 case *New York Times v. United States* played in our nation's judicial history.

Freedom of the press was shaped in an extraordinary stream of Supreme Court decisions that began with *Sullivan* in 1964 and continued through 1991 with *Cohen v. Cowles Media Company*. (*Sullivan* established the "actual malice" standard that has to be met before press reports about public officials or public figures can be considered to be defamed and libeled. It enabled the free reporting of the civil-rights campaigns in the southern United States and is one of the key decisions supporting the freedom of the press.) During this remarkable period of less than thirty years, the Court ruled in more than forty different cases involving the press and its right to function freely without undue influence or restraint from government. The Court examined obscure, rarely mentioned cases from the past, built upon them, and expanded upon them until today we are left with a solid body of groundbreaking decisions and a better understanding that the value of a free press plays in a free society.

Today, it is a given–the First Amendment, along with the Fourteenth Amendment (which guarantees all US citizens the rights and privileges of citizenship), allow not only freedom of speech, but also freedom of the press.

But in early US history, that was not the case. In fact, it took nearly one hundred fifty years after the adoption of the Bill of Rights, and the First Amendment along with it, for the Court to issue its first decision based solely upon the concept of freedom of the press.

In 1931, *Near v. Minnesota* ratified the concept that a prior restraint, or a legal prohibition against the press publishing something, is nearly always a violation of the First Amendment. *Near* is a landmark case, not only because it was the Court's first decision to invoke the press clause, but also because it established a fundamental concept within constitutional law. The concept says that, once the press obtains information that it believes is newsworthy, the government can rarely if ever prevent that information from being published.

This engraving depicts the trial of John Peter Zenger in 1734, which established the precedent for freedom of the press in the United States.

After the decision in *Near* (and before *Sullivan* in 1964), a handful of important cases came before the Court. In 1936, *Grosjean v. American Press Company* established the concept that governments may not impose taxes on a newspaper based upon its circulation, because doing so could be a means of controlling what is published through the penalties of taxation.

Two years later, in *Lovell v. City of Griffin* (1938), the Court overturned a city statute that made legal the imprisonment of a publisher for publishing material that the city found to be a "nuisance" or to be an offense against the city. The Court again cited the necessity of maintaining a totally free press uncontrolled by government interference.

In 1943, in *Largent v. Texas*, the Court once again upheld the sanctity of freedom of the press by striking down a law requiring that persons selling religious books and pamphlets (among other things) be required to first obtain a license from the Texas city of Paris. The law, according to the Court, placed an undue restraint upon freedom of the press, freedom of speech, and freedom of religion.

While these and similar cases helped continue to define and expand upon the Court's definition of freedom of the press, it was *New York Times v. Sullivan* in 1964 that crystallized the concept once and for all.

Sullivan, like *Near*, is a landmark Supreme Court case, and not because the Court's decision saved the *New York Times* from nearly certain bankruptcy when it decided to report the truth about civil-rights violations as they existed in the South. Much more than that, the decision was groundbreaking because it provided the Court with an opportunity to delve into the entire question of freedom of the press, and the Court responded by expanding the definition of the press clause itself.

The Court explained in *Sullivan* that freedom of the press includes not only the right to be free from *prior restraint* on publication, but also to be largely exempt from any punishment when it reports what it believes to be the truth about matters of public concern. That means, according to the Court, that its journalists should be free from imprisonment, that no criminal fines can be filed against a newspaper or its staff for doing what they believe to be their job, and that civil damages should not be paid to a plaintiff who files a defamation suit.[1]

In fact, when the subject of press scrutiny is a public official or some other public figure, the Court said in *Sullivan* that even a false statement is protected by the First Amendment unless it is a "calculated falsehood," a statement that a reporter or editor knows to be untrue or probably untrue but decides to publish anyway.

That gave a lot of leeway to publications that they did not enjoy before the Court's findings.[2]

Over the course of the quarter-century following *Sullivan,* the Court took it upon itself to explore the complexities of the case nearly yearly. During that period, the Court focused on the nature of the restraints designed to stifle freedom of the press as well as the extent to which the First Amendment protects the press from specific governmental actions.

In cases such as *Near* and the Pentagon Papers case from 1971, the Court established freedom of the press from previous restraints on publication as nearly absolute, giving the right for the press to publish information that even the president concluded would harm the national security, if not the movements of troopships at sea in time of war.

On the other hand, in 1974's *Miami Herald Publishing Company v. Tornillo,* the Court embraced the alternative position that the government has virtually no power to force the press to publish information that the press would prefer to leave unpublished.[3] Emerging as an extension of the Pentagon Papers case—but in reverse of what that Court's decision provided—the Court was clearly telling the government to back away from meddling in the affairs of the press.

At the same time, however, the Court decided that not all media are equal—that newspapers and radio or television news broadcasts, for example, are not all entitled to the same degree of protections based upon freedom of the press. The Court held that Congress and the Federal Communications Commission (FCC) may regulate the activities of broadcasters operating over "public" airwaves in a manner that would be a violation of the First Amendment if applied to newspapers. Take a look at the difference 1969's *Red Lion Broadcasting Company v. FCC* and *Tornillo*.

The Court's reasoning in *Red Lion*, in which it upheld the FCC's "Fairness Doctrine" and "personal attack" rule (the right of a person criticized on a broadcast station to respond to such criticism over the same airwaves licensed to that station) has never been denied, although the justices have expressly declined to extend it to other, later-developed communications media, including cable television (1994's *Turner Broadcasting v. FCC*) and the Internet (1997's *Reno v. American Civil Liberties Union*), to which the "scarcity" rationale for regulation does not apply.

Even in the broadcast context, however, *Sullivan* and the cases that followed it stand for the proposition that the First Amendment protects the publication of truthful information about matters of public concern. The press is protected not only from prior restraint, but also from subsequent punishment, at least in the absence of a clear need to vindicate a governmental interest of the "highest order." This formulation has come to be known as "the *Daily Mail* principle," after the Supreme Court's 1979 decision in *Smith v. Daily Mail Publishing Company*. In it, the Court held that a newspaper could not be liable for publishing the name of a juvenile offender in violation of a West Virginia law declaring such information to be private.[4]

The protections against subsequent punishments for reporting the truth afforded by the *Daily Mail* principle are not absolute, but the barriers to such government regulation of the press are set extremely high.

No Protection Against False Information

Sullivan and its companion cases (including *Gertz v. Robert Welch, Inc.*, an important libel case decided on the same day as *Tornillo* and that for some reason includes *Branzburg v. Hayes*, which involved the existence of a journalist's privilege under the First Amendment but had nothing to do with false information) also hold that the First Amendment protects the publication of false information about matters of public concern in a variety of contexts, although with considerably less enthusiasm than it defends publication of the truth. Even so, public officials and public figures may not recover civil damages for injury to their reputations unless they were the victims of a reckless disregard for truth in the dissemination of a "calculated falsehood."

In fact, private citizens may not collect civil damages for harm to their reputations caused by falsehoods relating to a matter of public concern unless the publisher's conduct violates a fault-based standard of care. Although expressions of "opinion" are not always immune from legal sanction, in its 1990 decision in *Milkovich v. Lorain Journal Company*, the Court held that statements that could not be proven false, or those that people might not assume are factual at all but merely "rhetorical hyperbole," are absolutely protected by the First Amendment.[5]

At the same time, the Supreme Court has not given a free pass to the press beyond denouncing *prior restraint* and legal sanctions prior to publication. In its 1978 decision *Zurcher v. Stanford Daily*, for example, the Court held that the First Amendment does not protect the press and its newsrooms from the issuance of otherwise valid search warrants. Similarly, in 1979's *Herbert v. Lando*, the Court concluded that the press clause does not extend to a journalist who declines to testify about the "editorial process" in a court of civil discovery.

Perhaps most importantly of all, in *Branzburg v. Hayes* (1972), a sharply divided Court refused to agree with the press that the First Amendment protects journalists from being forced to reveal the identities of their confidential sources, at least in the context of a grand-jury proceeding.

But, on the other hand, the Court has not addressed the issue of protected sources in the decades since its decision in *Branzburg* and has, in effect, allowed the lower courts to fashion an impressive body of law grounding just such a "reporter's privilege" firmly in the press clause itself. That privilege, though, is by no means absolute and may be forfeited in a variety of circumstances, especially when no confidential source is placed in jeopardy or when the disclosure of a source is being sought in a grand-jury or other criminal proceeding.

No Obvious Winner

As might be expected in so complex an area as freedom of the press, the Court has backed the press on some rights issues and backed away on others. It has found, for example, that the First Amendment protects the affirmative rights of the press to have access to at least some governmental proceedings. In a series of decisions beginning with 1980's *Richmond Newspapers, Inc. v. Virginia*, the Court established that the First Amendment protects not only the press from *prior restraint* and other government-imposed penalties, but also protects the public with a right to attend criminal trials and other judicial proceedings. On the other hand, the Court has ruled that this right is not absolute and may be balanced against other competing interests held by the proponents of secret proceedings advocating no press allowed.[6]

On the other hand, in cases such as 1975's *Cox Broadcasting Corporation v. Cohn*, the Court has explicitly recognized the role that the press plays as a "surrogate," or a stand-in, for the general public in gathering and publishing information on the public's behalf and for its benefit.

Yet, despite its protection of the press, the Court has taken great pains not to anoint the press with any more

First Amendment-based rights and immunities than those enjoyed by any solitary speaker, "lonely pamphleteer" (see *Branzburg v. Hayes*, 1972), or Internet chat-room participant.[7] The *New York Times* has no more rights under the constitution's freedom of press concept than does the person selling religious leaflets on the street corner.

In fact, the Court has rejected arguments advanced by the institutional press that, because of the important nature of its work in ensuring the free flow of ideas in a democratic society, it should be protected from still more laws that affect the general public. Only then can it remain unaffected by special-interest groups.

In an attempt to refine its position, the Court in 1991's *Cohen v. Cowles Media Company* expanded the definition of freedom of the press it had laid out in *Sullivan*. It emphasized that the press is properly subject to liability under the "generally applicable" law of contracts when it breaks a promise to keep a source's identity confidential, even when it does so in order to report truthful information about the source's involvement in a matter of public concern.

Revisiting the First Amendment

In the two decades since *Cohen*, the Court has been mostly quiet regarding the application of the First Amendment's protections to the institutional press. As the twenty-first century dawned, however, the Court briefly revisited the extent to which a "generally applicable" law, such as the federal wiretap statute, can constitutionally impose criminal penalties and civil liability on the press's publication of the contents of illegally recorded telephone conversations when that information is the truth and a matter of public concern.

In 2001 in *Bartnicki v. Vopper*, the Court held that, even when a statute is designed to discourage illegal conduct, such as intercepting private telephone conversations, and not to penalize the content of press reports, it still constitutes a "naked prohibition" on the publication of information by the press that is "fairly characterized as a regulation of pure speech" in violation of the First Amendment.[8]

In so holding, the Court ushered in a new century of First Amendment affirmations of both the *Daily Mail* principle (the fundamental right of a free press to publish truthful information about public matters) and the "central meaning of the First Amendment" on which it is based—*Sullivan's* recognition that the "freedom of expression upon public questions is secured by the First Amendment" so that "debate on public issues should be uninhibited, robust and wide-open."

The Bottom Line

While *Sullivan* and several dozen lesser related cases over the years have helped the Court to define what freedom of the press is and how it applies to everyday life, a much more specific, much more visible, much more highly controversial case—*New York Times v. United States*—was required to bring the entire question of freedom of the press to the foreground.

As the war in Vietnam raged on throughout the sixties and seventies, the *New York Times* saw an obligation to publish what it knew to be controversial findings it had obtained illegally about the war and the US government's involvement in that Southeastern Asian country's national affairs.

By forcing the case to the US Supreme Court and before the eyes of hundreds of millions of people around the world, the paper was determined to advance the Court's findings in *Sullivan* and to keep a nation's attention focused on a steadily expanding concept, one that our Founding Fathers had foreseen as critical to a free society in an otherwise hostile world: freedom of the press.

CHAPTER 9

Freedom of the Press in the New Millennium

ew freedom of the press visits to the US Supreme Court
have been made in the roughly two decades since the
year 2000. But at least two springing from the finding
in the *New York Times* case have made their way to the courts,
for good reason. Both involve clarifications of the freedoms
that the First Amendment grants to the press—no matter how
unpopular the reasons behind them may be.

The first—*United States v. Stevens*—was a 2010 decision by
the Supreme Court ruling that a federal statute making the
commercial production, sale, or possession of depictions of
cruelty to animals a crime. In its decision, the Court found
the law to be an unconstitutional abridgment of the First
Amendment right to freedom of speech.

The case involved Robert J. Stevens, an author and small-
time film producer who presented himself as an authority on

pit bulls. He collected and sold videotapes showing dogfights. Although he didn't participate in the fights himself, he received a 37-month sentence under a 1999 federal law that banned trafficking in "depictions of animal cruelty."[1]

District Court Proceedings

Public Law No: 106-152 was a federal criminal statute that prohibited the creation, sale, or possession of depictions of cruelty to animals for commercial gain. The law had been enacted in 1999 mostly to target so-called "crush videos" that showed people crushing small animals in order to gratify a sexual fetish. It excluded from prosecution "any depiction that has serious religious, political, scientific, educational, journalistic, historical, or artistic value."

In 2004, Robert Stevens was indicted for creating and selling three videotapes, two of which depicted pit bulls engaged in dog fighting. The third and more "gruesome" tape depicted a pit bull attacking a domestic pig as part of the dog being trained to catch and kill wild hogs. Although Stevens' criminal prosecution concerned only three tapes, he had made $20,000 in two and a half years by selling nearly 700 videos. Stevens was not accused of engaging in animal cruelty himself, nor of shooting the original footage from which the videos were created. However, the footage in each of the videos was "accompanied by introductions, narration, and commentary by Stevens, as well as accompanying literature of which Stevens is the author."

Stevens filed a motion to dismiss the indictment, arguing that the federal statute violated his right to freedom of speech under the First Amendment. The District Court denied his motion in November 2004. In January 2005, Stevens was convicted by a jury after a deliberation of 45 minutes.[2]

Third Circuit Decision

Stevens appealed, and the Third Circuit Court overturned his conviction, holding that 18 U.S.C. 48 violated his First Amendment right to free speech. The court stated that dog fighting, or the use of dogs to hunt hogs, may be made illegal to protect animals from cruelty, but such laws may not suspend a person's rights granted to Stevens under the First Amendment.

The government appealed, asking that the Supreme Court overturn the appellate court ruling. On April 20, 2009, the US Supreme Court agreed to review the lower court's decision. Oral arguments in the case were heard on October 6, 2009.

Stevens' attorney—Washington, DC, lawyer Patricia Millett—wrote:

The notion that Congress can suddenly strip a broad swath of never-before-regulated speech of First Amendment protection and send its creators to federal prison, based on nothing more than an ad hoc balancing of the "expressive value" of the speech against its "societal costs" is entirely alien to constitutional jurisprudence and a dangerous threat to liberty.

In June 2009, the Animal Legal Defense Fund (ALDF) filed a brief in defense of the animals' interests. The brief encouraged the Court to recognize the protection of animals as a compelling government interest and uphold Section 48.

More than a dozen media outlets joined an *amicus* brief (a brief containing arguments or recommendations that are filed by people or groups who are not directly involved in the case but have an interest in the outcome) in support of Stevens, including the *New York Times*, National Public Radio, the American Society of News Editors, the Association of Alternative Newsweeklies, Citizen Media Law Project, MediaNews Group, the National Press Photographers Association, the Newspaper Association of America, the Newspaper Guild–CWA, Outdoor Writers Association of America, the Radio-Television News Directors Association, the Society of Environmental Journalists, and the Society of Professional Journalists.[3]

The Supreme Court's Decision

On April 20, 2010, the Supreme Court affirmed the appellate court ruling in an 8–1 decision written by Chief Justice Roberts, with Justice Alito dissenting. The Court found that Section 48 was substantially overbroad and, thus, invalid under the First Amendment to the United States Constitution.

Justice Alito dissented, explaining, "[T]he most relevant of our prior decisions is Ferber, 458 U. S. 747, which concerned child pornography. The Court there held that child pornography is not protected speech, and I believe that *Ferber*'s reasoning dictates a similar conclusion here."[8]

On April 21, one day after the Supreme Court struck down the law, its original sponsor, Representative Elton Gallegly introduced a new bill with much more specific language indicating it was intended only to apply to "crush videos." President Barack Obama signed the bill into law on December 9, 2010.

A *New York Times'* Spin-Off

In a First-Amendment spin-off from the *New York Times v. United States*, Obsidian Finance Group—a financial advisory firm that was managing the bankruptcy proceedings of Summit 1031, a real-estate company—met with sharp Internet criticism. Crystal Cox was a self-proclaimed "investigative blogger." In her blogs, Cox accused Obsidian and its cofounder Kevin Padrick of committing tax fraud, paying off the media and politicians, intimidating and threatening whistleblowers, and engaging in various other illegal activities in their handling of the bankruptcy. Cox repeatedly claimed that her investigations would expose Obsidian and Padrick's corruption. In response, Obsidian and Padrick brought suit against Cox for defamation in the United States District Court for the District of Oregon, asserting that all of Cox's claims were false and that they had damaged Padrick's reputation.

At first, the court seemed to lean toward dismissing the defamation claims against Cox. To establish a defamation claim, the defamatory material had to assert a fact that could be proven true or false, as opposed to merely stating an opinion. The court held that even though Cox's allegations of fraud and corruption are technically assertions of fact, they appeared on several obviously biased blog sites, and Cox made no attempt to provide supporting evidence. The sites were strictly opinion-based.

The court ruled that, in the context of Cox's ranting blog posts, the allegations were unlikely to be taken as fact by any of her audience. As a result, the court held that Cox's right to voice her opinions was protected by the First Amendment and that her statements could not be considered defamation.

But, after reviewing several more blog posts, the court found one to be more factual in tone and content than the others. That blog detailed Summit's bankruptcy filing and tax liability, specifically accusing Obsidian and Padrick of lying on tax filings and stealing money. The court allowed the defamation claim on that one particular post to move forward.

A trial was held on November 29, 2011, and the jury ruled in favor of the plaintiffs, awarding Obsidian and Padrick $2.5 million in damages.

Opinion of the Court

After the trial, on November 30, 2011, the court issued an opinion clarifying some of its pre-trial oral rulings. Cox had claimed that her allegations against Obsidian and Padrick were based on evidence from a secret source, which she refused to name. Under Oregon's media shield laws, any person involved with a "medium of communication to the public" did not have to reveal the source of his or her information. The state defined "medium of communication" as "including but not limited to" a list of traditional modes of media, including newspapers, magazines, television, etc. The court held that, based on the facts of the case, Cox was not affiliated with any of the listed mediums, had no history of reliability as a journalist, and therefore did not qualify for the media shield laws.

Cox also claimed to have immunity under Oregon's retraction statutes, which say that general damages for defamation could only be awarded if the plaintiffs had asked for a retraction, which Padrick had not done. The court again held that Cox did not qualify because her blogs and practices did not fall under any of the traditional modes of media enumerated in the statute.

First Amendment Issues

Cox also asserted that because the plaintiffs are public figures and because she blogged about a matter of public concern, she was entitled to First Amendment protection. In order to prove defamation, then, actual malice on Cox's part would have had to be shown. "Actual malice" would have required that Cox had knowledge of the truth and knowingly disregarded the facts, instead of simply making a false assertion of the facts on her blog.

The court eventually held that neither Obsidian or Padrick were public figures, and Cox was the only person trying to publicize the issue. As a result, actual malice did not need to be proven by the plaintiffs.

Cox had also asserted that, even if the plaintiffs weren't public figures, in order for the plaintiffs to claim damages, they must prove actual malice because she is a "media" outlet. The court again held that Cox did not qualify as "media." In its reasoning, the court cited her lack of a journalism degree, lack of affiliation with traditional media outlets, lack of adherence to journalistic standards such as fact-checking and fair coverage, and the absence of Cox writing any original material rather than assembling the works of others. As such, the court found that the plaintiffs could seek damages without any further evidence of actual malice.

The holdings in the case ignited public debate over whether bloggers should be considered journalists and entitled to the same protections. Cox suggested that this case "should matter to everyone who writes on the Internet" and that if she "[doesn't] win [her] appeal, we all lose."

Padrick responded by saying, "The concept of media [would be] rendered worthless ... if anyone can self-proclaim themselves to be media." Padrick also pointed out the real damage done to his reputation and business by Cox and stated his belief that he would have won the case even if Cox had been considered "media."

The three-judge panel of the Ninth Circuit ruled that liability for a defamatory blog post involving a matter of public concern cannot be imposed without proof of fault and actual damages. Bloggers saying libelous things about private citizens concerning public matters can only be sued if they're negligent. The plaintiff must prove the defendant's negligence—the same standard that applies when news media are sued. In so ruling, the federal appellate court essentially said that journalists and bloggers are one and the same when it comes to the First Amendment. In the words of Eugene Volokh, a professor at the UCLA School of Law, the nonprofessional press, especially bloggers, "for First Amendment purposes, have the same rights as others do, as for example the institutional media does."

The unanimous three-judge panel had rejected the argument that the negligence standard established for private defamation actions by the US Supreme Court in *Gertz v. Robert Welch, Inc.* only applied to "the institutional [conventional] press."

"The *Gertz* court did not expressly limit its holding to the defamation of institutional media defendants," Judge Andrew Hurwitz wrote for the three-judge panel.

And, although the Supreme Court has never directly held that the *Gertz* rule applies beyond the institutional press, it has repeatedly refused in non-defamation contexts to accord greater First Amendment protection to the institutional media than to other speakers.

The protections of the First Amendment do not turn on whether [or not] the defendant was a trained journalist, formally affiliated with traditional news entities, engaged in conflict-of-interest disclosure, went beyond just assembling others' writings or tried to get both sides of a story. ... In defamation cases, the public-figure status of a plaintiff and the public importance of the statement at issue —not the identity of the speaker—provide the First Amendment touchstones.[3]

And so it was that a Supreme Court Decision in *New York Times* triggered a defining moment in the Ninth Circuit Court that helped define a question plaguing journalists, bloggers, and the general public for decades. Except for the groundwork laid in the *Times* case, we might *still* not have a definitive ruling on exactly who are journalists and precisely to what protections under the First Amendment they are entitled.

Will there be other court findings—at the Supreme Court level or below—similarly drawing from the landmark case? It would seem so. As time evolves and society changes, so do the means and technologies of communication. That means, by necessity, that the definitions associated with news reporters, journalists, and others charged with gathering and distributing the news may also change.

The Supreme Court, in its findings in *New York Times v. United States*, laid the groundwork for a wide range of decision regarding the press and its First Amendment rights. Where will the courts go from here?

That is a question that only the passage of time may answer.

Questions to Consider

1. Under what reasoning did the Nixon administration feel it had a right to withhold what it termed "classified information" from the public?

2. What is "prior restraint?"

3. Why are prior restraints rarely justified, even in matters of extreme government importance or national security?

4. Why did the *New York Times* believe the government was in violation of the First Amendment in preventing the publication of "classified information?"

5. How did the *New York Times* obtain copies of the documents the government claimed were top secret?

6. To which foreign country did the "Pentagon Papers" refer?

7. Under what circumstances, if any, may the government stop a newspaper from publishing material?

8. What other case did the Supreme Court decide along with *New York Times v. United States*?

9. What was the final vote in *New York Times v. United States*?

Primary Source Documents

In a 6-3 *per curiam* decision, the Supreme Court agreed with the two lower courts, which had originally decided that the government had not met its "heavy burden" of showing a justification for prior restraint. The court issued a very brief opinion, affirming that it concurred with the decisions of the two lower courts to reject the government's request for an injunction.

Mr. Justice Black, concurring.

"[T]he injunction against the *New York Times* should have been vacated without oral argument when the cases were first presented. … [E]very moment's continuance of the injunctions … amounts to a flagrant, indefensible, and continuing violation of the First Amendment. … When the Constitution was adopted, many people strongly opposed it because the document contained no Bill of Rights … In response to an overwhelming public clamor, James Madison offered a series of amendments to satisfy citizens that these great liberties would remain safe … In the First Amendment the Founding Fathers gave the free press the protection it must have to fulfill its essential role in our democracy. The press was to serve the governed, not the governors. The Government>s power to censor the press was abolished so that the press would remain forever free to censure the Government. The press was protected so that it could bare the secrets of government and inform the people. Only a free and unrestrained press can effectively expose deception in government. And paramount among the responsibilities of a free press is the duty to prevent any part of the government from deceiving the people and sending them off to distant lands to die of foreign fevers and foreign shot and shell. ... [W]e are asked to hold that ... the Executive Branch, the Congress, and the Judiciary can make laws ... abridging freedom of the press in the name of 'national security.' ... To find that the President has 'inherent power' to halt the publication of news ... would wipe out the First Amendment and destroy the fundamental liberty and security of the very people the Government hopes to make 'secure.' ... The word 'security' is a broad, vague generality whose contours should not be invoked to abrogate the fundamental law embodied in the First Amendment. The guarding of military and diplomatic secrets at the expense of informed representative government provides no real security ... The Framers of the First Amendment, fully aware of both the need to defend a new nation and the abuses of the English and Colonial governments, sought to give this new society strength and security by providing that freedom of speech, press, religion, and assembly should not be abridged."

Mr. Justice Douglas, concurring.

Agreeing largely with Black, Justice Douglas argued that the need for a free press as a check on government prevents any governmental restraint on the press.

"Secrecy in government is fundamentally anti-democratic, perpetuating bureaucratic errors. Open debate and discussion of public issues are vital to our national health. On public questions there should be 'uninhibited, robust, and wide-open' debate. … These [secret government] documents contain data concerning the communications system of the United States, the publication of which is made a crime. But the criminal sanction is not urged by the United States as the basis of equity power. … There are numerous sets of this material in existence and they apparently are not under any controlled custody. Moreover, the President has sent a set to the Congress. We start then with a case where there already is rather wide distribution of the material that is destined for publicity, not secrecy. I have gone over the material listed in the in-camera brief of the United States. It is all history, not future events. None of it is more recent than 1968."

Mr. Justice Brennan, concurring.

"[O]ur judgments in the present cases may not be taken to indicate the propriety, in the future, of issuing temporary stays and restraining orders to block the publication of material sought to be suppressed by the Government. So far as I can determine, never before has the United States sought to enjoin a newspaper from publishing information in its possession."

Mr. Justice Stewart, concurring.

Justice Potter Stewart (along with Justice Byron R. White) agreed that it is the responsibility of the Executive to ensure national security through the protection of its information. However, in areas of national defense and international affairs, the President of the United States possesses great constitutional independence that is virtually unchecked by the Legislative and Judicial branch.

In absence of governmental checks and balances, "The only effective restraint upon executive policy and power in [these two areas] may lie in an enlightened citizenry—in an informed and critical public opinion which alone can here protect the values of democratic government."

Mr. Justice White, concurring.

"I concur in today's judgments, but only because of the concededly extraordinary protection against prior restraints enjoyed by the press under our constitutional system. I do not say that in no circumstances would the First Amendment permit an injunction against publishing information about government plans or operations. Nor, after examining the materials the Government characterizes as the most sensitive and destructive, can I deny that revelation of these documents will do substantial damage to public interests. Indeed, I am confident that their disclosure will have that result. But I nevertheless agree that the United States has not satisfied the very heavy burden that it must meet to warrant an injunction against publication in these cases, at least in the absence of express and appropriately limited congressional authorization for prior restraints in circumstances such as these."

Mr. Justice Marshall, concurring.

"The Government contends that the only issue in these cases is whether in a suit by the United States, the First Amendment bars a court from prohibiting a newspaper from publishing material whose disclosure would pose a 'grave and immediate danger to the security of the United States.' With all due respect, I believe the ultimate issue in these cases is even more basic than the one posed by the Solicitor General. The issue is whether this Court or the Congress has the power to make law. ... I believe that the judgment of the

United States Court of Appeals for the District of Columbia Circuit should be affirmed and the judgment of the United States Court of Appeals for the Second Circuit should be reversed insofar as it remands the case for further hearings."

In writing dissenting opinions, Chief Justice Burger and Justices Harlan and Blackmun wrote the following:

Mr. Chief Justice Burger, dissenting.

When "the imperative of a free and unfettered press comes into collision with another imperative, the effective functioning of a complex modern government" there should be a detailed study on the effects of these actions. He argued that in the haste of the proceedings, and given the size of the documents, the Court was unable to gather enough information to make a decision. He also argued that the *Times* should have discussed the possible societal repercussions with the government prior to publication of the material. The chief justice did not argue that the government had met the aforementioned standard, but rather that the decision should not have been made so hastily.

Mr. Justice Harlan, dissenting.

"With all respect, I consider that the Court has been almost irresponsibly feverish in dealing with these cases. ... Both the Court of Appeals for the Second Circuit and the Court of Appeals for the District of Columbia Circuit rendered judgment on June 23. The *New York Times'* petition for certiorari, its motion for accelerated consideration thereof, and its application for interim relief were filed in this Court on June 24 at about 11 a.m. ... The briefs of the parties were received less than two hours before argument on June 26. ... This frenzied train of events took place in the name of the presumption against prior restraints created by the First Amendment. Due regard for the extraordinarily important and difficult questions involved in these litigations should have led the Court to shun such a precipitate timetable. ... Pending further hearings in each case conducted under the appropriate ground rules, I would continue the restraints on publication. I cannot believe that the doctrine prohibiting prior restraints reaches to the point of preventing courts from maintaining the status quo long enough to act responsibly in matters of such national importance as those involved here."

Mr. Justice Blackmun, dissenting.

"If ... damage has been done, and if, with the Court's action today, these newspapers proceed to publish the critical documents and there results therefrom 'the death of soldiers, the destruction of alliances, the greatly increased difficulty of negotiation with our enemies, the inability of our diplomats to negotiate,' to which list I might add the factors of prolongation of the war and of further delay in the freeing of United States prisoners, then the Nation's people will know where the responsibility for these sad consequences rests [with the US Supreme Court]."

Chronology

1971 The *New York Times* obtains a 1968 top-secret 7,000-page study of the US military intervention in Vietnam. Produced by the Department of Defense, the *History of U.S. Decision Making Process on Viet Nam Policy* revealed major US military errors and political cover-ups regarding America's involvement in the War in Vietnam.

June 13, 1971 After analyzing the documents (better known as the "Pentagon Papers") for several months, the *Times* begins publishing a series of articles about the revelations contained within the papers.

June 15, 1971 After the *Times* has published its first installment of articles, President Richard M. Nixon tells Secretary of State Henry Kissinger to have the Justice Department get an injunction to prevent the *Times* from publishing any additional installments. The next day, the Department of Justice obtains a restraining order prohibiting further publication.

June 18, 1971 The *New York Times* files suit to have the restraining order lifted, and after a series of complicated legal maneuverings, the issue is forwarded to the US Supreme Court for further consideration.

June 26, 1971 The Supreme Court hears oral arguments in *New York Times v. United States*.

June 30, 1971 The US Supreme Court announces its decision in the Pentagon Papers cases. In a *per curiam* decision, the Court rules that the government did not meet its burden for a prior restraint under the First Amendment. Three justices dissent, arguing that the Court rushed to judgment and thus endangered national security.

Chapter Notes

Chapter 1. The Vietnam War

1. Stanley Karnow, *Vietnam: A History* (New York, NY: Viking, 1991), p. 264.
2. Ibid., p. 267.
3. Ibid.
4. Ibid., p. 269.
5. Ibid., p. 335.
6. Ibid., p. 339.
7. Ibid., p. 606.
8. Ibid., p. 607.
9. Richard Reeves, *President Nixon: Alone in the White House* (New York, NY: Simon and Schuster, 2002), p. 80.
10. Council on Foreign Relations, *The United States in World Affairs* (Ann Arbor, MI: University of Michigan, 1970), p. 126.

Chapter 2. The Pentagon Papers

1. Meyer Berger, "The Gray Lady Reaches 100," *Life*, September 17, 1951.
2. "The New York Times," Encyclopedia Britannica, www.britannica.com/topic/The-New-York-Times.

3. *New York Times*, June 15, 1971, p. 1.

4. Ibid., p. 18.

5. Ibid.

6. Ibid.

7. Ibid.

8. Ibid.

9. Stanley Karnow, *Vietnam: A History* (New York, NY: Viking, 1991), p. 647.

Chapter 3. A Case for the Government

1. Stanley Karnow, *Vietnam: A History* (New York, NY: Viking, 1991), p. 648.

2. Ibid.

3. Ibid.

4. Ibid., p. 649.

5. *New York Times Company et al. v. United States of America* (Preliminary Statement, US District Court, Southern District of New York, June 15, 1971), pp. 1–2.

6. *New York Times Company et al. v. United States of America* (Argument, US District Court, Southern District of New York, 71 Civ. 2662, June 15, 1971), pp. 3–7.

7. "Judge, at Request of U.S., Halts Times Vietnam Series Four Days Pending Hearing on Injunction," *New York Times*, June 16, 1971, p. 1–1.

8. *New York Times Company et al. v. United States of America* (Memorandum from US District Judge Murray I. Gurfein, June 15, 1971), pp. 2–3.

9. "Judge, at Request of U.S., Halts Times Vietnam Series," p. 1–1.

10. *New York Times Company et al. v. United States of America* (Affidavit of James L. Greenfield, US District Court, Southern District of New York, 71 Civ. 2662, June 18, 1971), pp. 3–4.

11. *New York Times Company et al. v. United States of America* (Oral Arguments, US District Court, Southern District of New York, 71 Civ. 2662, June 19, 1971), p. 17.

12. Ibid., pp. 31–32.

13. Ibid., pp. 71–72.

14. Ibid., p. 103.

15. Ibid., p. 112.

16. Ibid., p. 113.

Chapter 4. The *New York Times* Responds

1. *New York Times Company et al. v. United States of America* (Oral Arguments, US District Court, Southern District of New York, 71 Civ. 2662, June 19, 1971), pp. 22–24.

2. Ibid.

3. Ibid., pp. 28–29.

4. *New York Times Company et al. v. United States of America* (Opinion, US District Court, Southern District of New York, 71 Civ. 2662, June 19, 1971), p. 16.

5. *New York Times Company et al. v. United States of America* (Application for Vacatur of Stay, US Supreme Court, June 24, 1971), pp. 8–9.

6. *New York Times Company et al. v. United States of America* (Order, US Supreme Court, No. 1873, June 25, 1971).

Chapter 5. Before the Supreme Court

1. Fred P. Graham, "Supreme Court Agrees to Rule on Printing of Vietnam Series: Arguments to Be Heard Today," *New York Times*, June 26, 1971, pp. 1–10.

2. *New York Times*, June 27, 1971, p. 24.

3. Ibid.

4. Ibid.

5. Ibid., p. 25.

6. Ibid.

7. Ibid.

8. Ibid.

9. Ibid., pp. 25–26.

10. Ibid., p. 26.

11. Ibid.

12. Ibid.

13. Ibid.

Chapter 6. A Quick Decision

1. Fred P. Graham, "Supreme Court Weighs Issues on Vietnam Series After Pleas: Rejects a U.S. Secrecy Request," *New York Times*, June 27, 1971, p. 27.

2. *New York Times Company et al. v. United States of America* (Per Curiam Opinion, US Supreme Court, June 30, 1971), p. 1.

3. *New York Times Company et al. v. United States of America* (Dissenting opinions, Justices Burger, Blackmun, and Harlan, US Supreme Court, June 30, 1971).

4. *New York Times Company et al. v. United States of America* (Majority Opinions, June 30, 1971).

5. *New York Times Company et al. v. United States of America* (Opinion of Justice Black, June 30, 1971), p. 4.

6. *New York Times Company et al. v. United States of America* (Opinion of Justice Douglas, June 30, 1971), pp. 4–5.

7. *New York Times Company et al. v. United States of America* (Opinion of Justice Stewart, June 30, 1971), p. 4.

8. *New York Times Company et al. v. United States of America* (Opinion of Justice Marshall, June 30, 1971), p. 3.

9. Fred P. Graham, "Supreme Court, 6–3, Upholds Newspapers on Publication of the Pentagon Report," *New York Times*, July 1, 1971, p. 1–15.

10. Ibid.

11. Ibid., p. 1.

Chapter 7. A Free Press
There are no notes.

Chapter 8. A Far-Reaching Concept

1. *New York Times Company v. Sullivan*, 376 U.S. 254 (1964), pp. 265–292.

2. Ibid.

3. *Miami Herald Publishing Company v. Tornillo*, 418 U.S. 241 (1974), p. 244.

4. *Smith v. Daily Mail Publishing Company*, 443 U.S. 97 (1979), pp. 101–104.

5. *Milkovich v. Lorain Journal Company*, 497 U.S. 1 (1990), p. 497.

6. *Richmond Newspapers, Inc. v. Virginia*, 448 U.S. 555 (1980), pp. 563–575.

7. *Branzburg v. Hayes*, 408 U.S. 665 (1972), p. 408.

8. *Bartnicki et al. v. Vopper, AKA Williams, et al.*, 532 U.S. 514, p. 526.

Chapter 9. Freedom of the Press in the New Millennium

1. Adam Liptak, "Supreme Court Rejects Ban on Animal Cruelty Videos," *New York Times*, April 20, 2010.

2. Paula Reed Ward, "Animal Cruelty Case Pushed to Top Court," *Pittsburgh Post-Gazette*, December 17, 2008.

3. Eriq Gardner, "Bloggers Get First Amendment Protections in Defamation Lawsuits," *Hollywood Reporter*, January 17, 2014.

Glossary

affidavit A sworn statement made in writing.

amendment A change to an existing agreement or rule.

bill A proposal that could become a law if it is passed by the House of Representatives and the Senate and is signed by the president.

Bill of Rights The first ten amendments to the United States constitution.

certiorari A legal document issued by a superior court to an inferior court.

concurring opinion An opinion written by a judge or judges who agree with the majority opinion but hold a different reason for their view(s).

contention A point that is maintained in a legal proceeding.

criminal trial A trial of someone accused of crimes against the state.

dissenting opinion An opinion written by a judge or judges who disagree with the majority opinion.

evidence Something that is offered up as proof during a legal proceeding.

federal Having to do with the central (national) form of government, as opposed to a state or local government.

per curiam Latin phrase meaning "by the court."

petition A formal, official request.

precedent Prior legal decisions that establish a foundation for future decisions.

ratify To give official approval.

stay Suspension of a procedure by judicial or executive order.

unconstitutional In violation of either the US Constitution or state constitution.

United States Constitution The basic law forming the US government. It consists of seven articles and twenty-seven amendments.

United States Supreme Court A judicial body comprised of nine justices. As the highest court in the United States, it holds final say over whether or not a law is constitutional.

Further Reading

Books

Lebovic, Sam. *Free Speech and Unfree News: The Paradox of Press Freedom in America*. Cambridge, MA: Harvard University Press, 2016.

Prados, John, and Margaret Pratt Porter. *Inside the Pentagon Papers*. Lawrence, KS: University Press of Kansas, 2005.

Uncredited. *New York Times Company v. United States - Unabridged*. Audiobook, 2014.

Weaver, Russell. *Understanding the First Amendment*. Fifth Edition. Irvine, CA: LexisNexis, 2014.

Websites

Cornell University Law School

www.law.cornell.edu/supct/html/historics/USSC_CR_0403_0713_ZS.html

A transcript of the the *New York Times v. United States* case.

The National Security Archive, The George Washington University

www.gwu.edu/~nsarchiv/NSAEBB/NSAEBB48/supreme.html

Commentary and transcription of the *New York Times v. United States* case.

Oyez IIT Chicago-Kent College of Law

www.oyez.org/cases/1970-1979/1970/1970_1873/

A summary of the *New York Times v. United States* case with audio recording of the oral arguments.

Index